THE

A FIVE-STRIDIN' VALENTINE
BY ROLIN JONES

★

★

DRAMATISTS
PLAY SERVICE
· INC.

THE JAMMER
Copyright © 2008, Rolin Jones

All Rights Reserved

SPECIAL NOTE

SPECIAL NOTE ON SONGS AND RECORDINGS

For Kevin Rich

AUTHOR'S NOTE

Somewhere in the headstrong city of Kenosha, Wisconsin, resides a man named Kevin Rich. Unassuming, barely registering in the landscape, he stands no more than five feet nine inches. He has the arms of a T-Rex and a face that makes a compelling argument for mandatory birth control. In short, Kevin Rich is no David Beckham. But the kid can act up a storm. And *The Jammer* was written for him. And as much as I'd like Kevin Rich to suit up as Jack Lovington in every production of *The Jammer*, I think his married-far-beneath-her wife wouldn't approve.

So this is for you brave directors out there who have set aside *Long Day's Journey into Night*, stepped over *Arcadia*, kicked your Carol Churchill–loving Board of Directors to the curb, and decided to produce *The Jammer*.

Find your town's Kevin Rich. Oh, he's out there. Banging the side of a soda machine. Sitting at the end of the bar watching his ball team get their ass handed to them. In the elevator checking to see if his underwear still has elastic. When you find him, give that man a job. And after that load up the van with the seven or eight other misfits who've been passed over for Othello, or Blanche, or Prior and drive them joyfully to the taco stand that is this play. I promise you … they will all end up sleeping with each other.

What else? The play is set in 1958. The Beatles have not landed. Keep the music sandwiched between Perry Como and primitive dining-hall rock 'n' roll. The play is also fast. If it clocks in at over ninety minutes, blow your whistle, take a lap and start again.

Last thoughts? Buy a copy of Keith Coppage's loving and exhaustive tome, *Roller Derby to Roller Jam*. Everything you need to know about the derby is housed within those pages. And don't spend too much money on everything else. It's a cheap date. Save your dimes and quarters for the bartender afterwards. She's a good gal and lives off her tips.

All other complaints, call the landlord.

—*Rolin Jones*

THE JAMMER was presented by Dwight Street Book Club & Hucklebee Consulting Group, as a part of the 2004 New York International Fringe Festival, which is a production of The Present Company. It was directed by Greg Felden; the set design was by Sandra Goldmark; the costume design was by Anne Kenney; the lighting design was by Scott Bolman; the choreography was by Tim Acito; the dramaturgy was by Christie Evangelisto; and the sound design was by Daniel Baker. The cast was as follows:

JACK LOVINGTON .... Kevin Rich
LINDY BATELLO .... Jeanine Serralles
FATHER KOSCIUSKO .... James Reynolds
LENNY RINGLE .... Billy Eugene Jones
BERT FEINBERG .... Jason Lindner
CHARLIE HEARTBREAK .... Peter Macon
BETH NUTTERMAN .... Gabrielle Castellin
CINDY GUMS .... Keiko Yamamoto
FATHER DOMINGO.................................... Andrew Guillarte

THE JAMMER was first presented by Spankin' Yanks as part of the 2004 Edinburgh Fringe Festival, directed by Gordon Carver and produced by Judith Hansen.

CHARACTERS

JACK LOVINGTON, early 30s

LINDY BATELLO, late 30s

LENNY RINGLE, 40s, African-American

FATHER KOSCIUSKO, JERRY "THREE NUTS" KIGER, TRACK MEDICAL ATTENDANT, 40s

BETH NUTTERMAN, AURORA, BUS DRIVER, early 30s

CHARLIE HEARTBREAK, DR. SEYMOUR FRIEDMAN, OLICE STRAYHORN, BENNIE THE DISPATCHER, ANGRY ROLLER COASTER RIDER, early 30s, African-American

BERT FINEBERG, AL DEEPADOVA, RIDE OPERATOR, 40s

FATHER DOMINGO, SPECS MACEDO, FAN IN THE CROWD, 20s/early 30s, Hispanic

CINDY GUMS, MRS. YOJIMBO, NURSE, SCARED KID ON ROLLERCOASTER, 20s, Asian-American

PLACE

Bushwick, Brooklyn and other cities along the Eastern Seaboard.

TIME

1958.

NOTE: Author's on-his-knees request: The roller derby sequences require an imaginative dance-like theatrical solution. They should be as visceral and violent as the rest of the play is dreamy. Please, please, please no actual roller skating! Thank you.

THE JAMMER

A rainy day in Bushwick, Brooklyn, 1958. A confessional inside Saint Barbara's Cathedral. There is a bucket just outside of the confessional. We hear the sound of a drip hitting the bucket. Father Kosciusko is just settling in. Jack Lovington sits in confession, holding a bag of groceries and an umbrella. He is out of breath.

JACK LOVINGTON. Forgive me Father for I have sinned. It's been eight hours since my last confession.

FATHER KOSCIUSKO. Just give me a second here, son. Have to get the ol' collar on …

JACK LOVINGTON. Thank you, Father, I'm having a real bad day and my insides are going crazy and I didn't know what else to do and I needed to talk to someone …

FATHER KOSCIUSKO. There's a new leak near the organ, all these buckets everywhere.

JACK LOVINGTON. … and Aurora was busy arranging the carnations for the Gilmartin funeral when I calls her at the florist and tells her, well …

FATHER KOSCIUSKO. Father Domingo's too busy with his pigeons …

JACK LOVINGTON. … I tells her I'm gonna pick up another shift in the yellow cab and she says you gone out in the cab five times this week and when are you gonna spend some time home. And I says I'll bring home some cold cuts and beer late night, and she says what you wanna do, bust our icebox or something? We got enough cold cuts thank you very much.

FATHER KOSCIUSKO. *(His collar on.)* Slow down.

JACK LOVINGTON. And so she slams down the phone, Father, and I go and clock out but I feel just awful 'cause I was lying, 'cause I ain't been driving the cab, I been going to the roller rink instead 'cause it's better than going home and listening to Aurora start in on me about how long we been engaged for …

FATHER KOSCIUSKO. You need to breathe.

JACK LOVINGTON. … 'cause I hear that and it ain't no more than five seconds before my lungs got a piece of newspaper string tied around them and some jerk's on the other end yanking it all tight-like. *(Jack starts hyperventilating.)*

FATHER KOSCIUSKO. Well perhaps you should have waited until you were married before you moved in with her … breathe, Jack.

JACK LOVINGTON. I ran here all the way from the grocery store.

FATHER KOSCIUSKO. We do not RUN into God's house like we're a dog.

JACK LOVINGTON. Sorry, Father.

FATHER KOSCIUSKO. God doesn't listen to dogs.

JACK LOVINGTON. Yes, Father.

FATHER KOSCIUSKO. Dogs are godless, Jack. That's why they eat dog food.

JACK LOVINGTON. I can't feel my hands.

FATHER KOSCIUSKO. Now, Jack, this house is always open for you. You know that. There's no need to run. So tell me. *Slowly.* What's troubling you? *(Father Kosciusko begins to take off his shoes.)*

JACK LOVINGTON. Father, I don't want to marry Aurora no more.

FATHER KOSCIUSKO. You told me that this morning, Jack. *(Father Kosciusko rolls his socks into a ball.)*

JACK LOVINGTON. No, I said I *think* I don't. But that wasn't true and I knew that all day at work, Father. This morning, I wanted to tell you but I forgot it wasn't Sunday when she's standing right outside and listening to what I tell you.

FATHER KOSCIUSKO. I'm sure that's not true. *(Father Kosciusko leans out the confessional and puts the socks in the bucket, ending the drip noise.)*

JACK LOVINGTON. She overheard me talking about the impure acts two weeks ago. I gotta open the door when I go to the bathroom now.

FATHER KOSCIUSKO. I see.

JACK LOVINGTON. I got trouble going to the bathroom when someone's looking at me.

FATHER KOSCIUSKO. We all do, my son.

JACK LOVINGTON. And you know, Father, I guess I can get used to that but it's just she's all heavy about me working at the cardboard factory saying Al Deepadova ain't got no problem working at the factory. And I says yeah, well he don't work the night shift in the yellow cab. And she says you don't have to work at the yellow cab, we got enough money with me working at the florist.

FATHER KOSCIUSKO. There are always compromises in a relationship. There are always disagreements.

JACK LOVINGTON. Father, it's a man's job to make the money. I tells her that and she says, yeah, well I'm a modern woman. And I says it still ain't enough money 'cause we're still like the rest of them. Going to the picture show with all the kids running up and down the aisles 'cause we can't afford nothing but the matinee. And she says maybe we could afford a decent picture if I wasn't spending the money at the Armory, watching the derby.

FATHER KOSCIUSKO. Aurora's a God-fearing woman.

JACK LOVINGTON. But Father I tell her how much I like the derby. I tell her I got talent. And she says, yeah, you're a regular Jack Benny. No, I say, I got *skating* talent! I tells her I can skate faster than most of those guys out there, twice as fast, like I got fireworks on my feet, Father! And how I think in some way, God wants me to be a racer.

FATHER KOSCIUSKO. The derby's a godless place.

JACK LOVINGTON. She said you were gonna say that. But I got proof says otherwise, Father.

FATHER KOSCIUSKO. Proof?

JACK LOVINGTON. I got a sign from God today, Father.

FATHER KOSCIUSKO. A sign? *(Jack takes out a piece of cardboard that looks like it was ripped off the side of a packing box.)*

JACK LOVINGTON. I was flipping the boxes, wrapping them up in the plastic, breathing in all them dust flakes like I do everyday when suddenly this one box I'm holding gets all tingly and it shoots out of my hands and goes clear across the room near one of the windows! I look around to see if Al's seen what happened but he was just flipping and wrapping. So I goes over to it and I see the light from outside the window shining on it and that's when I see the word. *(Jack flips over the piece, revealing the word "skate" crudely carved into the cardboard. It's pathetic.)*

FATHER KOSCIUSKO. Let me see that. *(Jack hands it across to Father Kosciusko.)*

JACK LOVINGTON. It's a sign, Father. *(There is a long pause.)*

FATHER KOSCIUSKO. Jack Lovington?

JACK LOVINGTON. Yes?

FATHER KOSCIUSKO. Did you carve the word "skate" into this

piece of cardboard?

JACK LOVINGTON. Huh?

FATHER KOSCIUSKO. Jack?

JACK LOVINGTON. *(Pause.)* Yes.

FATHER KOSCIUSKO. Jack, come outside with me! *(They both exit the confessional, Jack holding his groceries and Father Kosciusko the cardboard.)* You don't have to be scared to come here. You don't have to fear my judgment.

JACK LOVINGTON. I met a man at the roller rink.

FATHER KOSCIUSKO. So that's what this is about.

JACK LOVINGTON. His name is Lenny Ringle. He said I had a nice five-stride.

FATHER KOSCIUSKO. Is that what they're calling it these days? Look, Jack, you're not alone. You don't need to draw up diversionary signs from God because you fell in love with a man.

JACK LOVINGTON. What?

FATHER KOSCIUSKO. It's a test the Lord puts his most attractive men up to.

JACK LOVINGTON. I'm not in love with Lenny. He wants me to skate for his roller derby team.

FATHER KOSCIUSKO. Say again.

JACK LOVINGTON. Yeah. He's been scouting for the Roller Derby League. He's been watching me and said I should work out with one of the teams. And I did! All this week! And now he wants me to suit up for the Jersey City Johnnies tonight at the Armory and it's gonna be on the television and I guess I just wanted your blessing, Father.

FATHER KOSCIUSKO. So you still want to marry Aurora?

JACK LOVINGTON. Of course I do. I'm sorry about lying to you, Father.

FATHER KOSCIUSKO. Yes, well, why don't we just forget this conversation ever happened?

JACK LOVINGTON. Okay.

FATHER KOSCIUSKO. Good. I absolve you. Now look. About Aurora. Women complain. They do it better than anyone else. However, the fact of the matter is a woman keeps a man consistent. Without Woman, Man would be a wanderer. Do you want to wander, Jack?

JACK LOVINGTON. Where would I be going?

FATHER KOSCIUSKO. No, Jack, you don't. Jack, I want you to go home, right this minute. I want you to bring her the cold cuts and the beer. I want you to look into her eyes and find that beautiful thing you saw in her years ago.

JACK LOVINGTON. But what about the ...

FATHER KOSCIUSKO. And when you see that beautiful thing I want you to tell her how important this roller race is to you. I want you to tell her what you told me here right now.

JACK LOVINGTON. I've tried ...

FATHER KOSCIUSKO. I want you to tell her about the feet of fire.

JACK LOVINGTON. Father.

FATHER KOSCIUSKO. Tell her about the fire!

JACK LOVINGTON. Okay.

FATHER KOSCIUSKO. After that, tell her you love her and that you'll be back before eleven o'clock.

JACK LOVINGTON. Then I got your blessing, Father?

FATHER KOSCIUSKO. You do.

JACK LOVINGTON. Thanks, Father! *(Jack exits with his groceries, leaving Father Kosciusko holding the "sign from god." We hear music creeping up in the background.)*

FATHER KOSCIUSKO. *(Calling out.)* It's a godless place, the Armory. Enter with God, Jack! Enter with God! *(Lights out. The music grows louder, enveloping the audience like a sweaty cloud. A raw, murky rock 'n' roll instrumental with a dirty rhythm guitar and a wailing saxophone. We see Bert Fineberg, holding a microphone, doing strange mouth-stretching exercises. His partner, Larry Calloway, is a cut-out TV commentator.)*

FIFTIES TV ANNOUNCER VOICE. It's time ... for Roller Derby! America's fastest growing ... most exciting sport! ... Roller Derby! All the thrills and spills you've come to expect from your favorite television show, the Roller Derby! Sponsored by Bluto Beer. When you've got a case of the "Oh no, not agains," grab a case of Bluto. Bluto Beer, the beer you can count on! Take it away, Bert Fineberg! *(Bert Fineberg snaps to attention, and we see on the stage two Brown Devils and one Johnnie skating their guts out! The rest of the teams are filled out by cut-out skaters moved around by members of the female cast dressed in black. A referee skates on the outside of the pack, a whistle in his mouth.)*

BERT FINEBERG. Bert Fineberg and Larry Calloway back with you live TRACKSIDE at the Coney Island Armory with time running out on the eighth and final period of tonight's match between the Jersey City Johnnies and the Brooklyn Brown Devils! And if you've just tuned in folks, TOO BAD!

BROWN DEVIL #1. Come on, boys, let's get the skinny one.

BERT FINEBERG. Words can't possibly encapsulate the back and forth, life and death, bombastic battle of interstate rivals, can they Larry? *(Brown Devil #2 smacks the "skinny" cut-out Johnnie off the track. Larry doesn't speak.)*

BROWN DEVIL #1. See ya on the other side, cupcake!

BERT FINEBERG. Oh boy, another Johnnie pivot skater knocked off the track tells a tale told once too often tonight, skate fans! We're all locked-in thirty-six to thirty-two, it's Brooklyn's match to lose. One minute, forty seconds left on the clock.

BROWN DEVIL #2. Clear out the high bank.

BROWN DEVIL #1. You heard the man, boys, drive 'em down! Drive 'em down! *(The Brown Devils form a wedge and begin to block the Johnnies down track, leaving a gaping hole upside the track!)*

BERT FINEBERG. Brooklyn blockers trying to wedge the Johnnies to the bottom ramp! Brown Devils surely winning the battle of the pack tonight, wouldn't you say Larry?! *(No response from Larry.)*

BROWN DEVIL #2. Rookie coming up from behind!

BROWN DEVIL #1. I can't see him, yet.

BROWN DEVIL #2. Watch it! *(Suddenly, Jack Lovington appears out of nowhere to whiz past the Brown Devil jammer and then past the pack. The referee signals the beginning of a jam as the pack fades to the back of the stage!)*

BERT FINEBERG. WHOA NELLIE, skate fans! Here comes Jack Lovington! It's been that way, folks, every time we sense a shadow swamping the Johnnies, OUT like a bolt of lighting comes the demon colt jammer!

BROWN DEVIL #1. Who is this guy?

BROWN DEVIL #2. I don't know but he sure is fast.

JOHNNIE # 2. Go get 'em, Jackie boy! *(Jack Lovington looks behind, gives his teammate a thumbs up and skates offstage. The pack races upstage again.)*

BERT FINEBERG. Lovington's accounted for half of the Johnnies' points tonight. Sweeping in and out of every errant fist the Devils have thrown at him! Begging the question, just how did this homegrown killer get away from the eyes of management? Larry? *(No response.)* Larry doesn't know. I don't know either! But someone up in the Brown Devils scouting office better find out 'cause this young man has turned what should have been a cakewalk into cakenightmare! *(A lady Brown Devil, Beth Nutterman, has slipped in between Bert and Larry.)*

BETH NUTTERMAN. Hey Bertie.

BERT FINEBERG. We're joined now by one of the Lady Brown Devils, Beth Nutterman. Beth, what's going on here tonight?

BETH NUTTERMAN. I don't know, Bert. Us girls did our part, but our guys are having a heck of a time out there.

BERT FINEBERG. Do you know anything about the new kid, Lovington?

BETH NUTTERMAN. I don't know nothing about him, and I don't care nothing about him, all I care's about is …

FAN IN THE CROWD. Take off your shirt, Nutterman!

BETH NUTTERMAN. Who said that?! Who's the jerk?!

FAN IN THE CROWD. Over here, babydoll. *(A flashbulb goes off, blinding Beth and Bert momentarily.)*

FAN IN THE CROWD. Thanks, tutz.

BETH NUTTERMAN. Crummy bum.

BERT FINEBERG. A colorful crowd here tonight and every night at the Armory! Great skating tonight, Beth.

BETH NUTTERMAN. Thanks Bertie. Keep your hands off the merchandise, Larry. *(Beth exits.)*

BERT FINEBERG. Remember, skate fans, we can't possibly show you everything on TV, so come on down and grab a Bluto and experience the derby LIVE! Plenty of good seats every time. *(The referee signals a warning to a Brown Devil. Suddenly Jack Lovington appears in the back of the stage again, skating like a crazy man, fighting off the jammer he bumped off the last time around.)* The referee gives a warning for unnecessary roughness. The clock's down to twenty seconds and WHOA NELLIE! Here comes Lovington again. Can you believe this kid?!

JOHNNIE #2. Gotta make a move!

JOHNNIE #1. I'll fall back.

JOHNNIE #2. Do it! *(Johnnie #1 fades back, puts his hand back.)*

BERT FINEBERG. Jersey City, sending a blocker back. Looks like they're going for a whip! Lovington's locked hands. And look out Bensonhurst! *(Jack takes his hand and gets whipped forward. Johnnie #1 throws a block, and one by one, flesh and cut-out alike, Jack Lovington passes all five Brown Devils.)* He passes one. He passes TWO. A THIRD Brown Devil. Oh my a devastating block and they got FOUR points … three seconds left. Two seconds, one second, HE'S DONE IT! HE'S DONE IT! LOVINGTON'S DONE IT! *(The referee blows the whistle, indicates five points. The Brown Devils take off their helmets in disgust. Skate off. The other Johnnies throw their hands up in celebration, Jack Lovington looks around, confused, then gets it. He smiles, the picture of sportsmanship. His teammates mob him at the railing.)* Jersey City thirty-seven, the Brooklyn Brown Devils thirty-six in one of the most spectacular spectacles this reporter has ever reported! A star is born in Brooklyn, ladies and gentlemen. A blinding bright star, indeed. Holy Christmas, Mr. Eisenhower! For Larry Calloway and all good people at Bluto Beer, this is Bert Fineberg saying thanks for tuning in, New York. See you next week at ... THE ROLLER DERBY! *(Lights down on Bert, Jack and the Johnnies. Lights up on Lenny Ringle, at a pay phone.)*

LENNY RINGLE. Is this Bushwick Yellow Cab? *(Listens.)* Good, I need a car to come pick me up on the corner of Knickerbocker and Central. *(Listens.)* Wherever I tell him, know what I mean? *(Listens.)* Right, as directed. And dispatch, I want to request one of your drivers. Yeah, I want Lovington. Jack Lovington. *(Listens.)* I don't care. I'll wait. Corner of Knickerbocker and Central, right in front of the Orthodox temple. Yeah, I'm getting fitted for a yarmulke, ya jerk, just get me the car. *(He hangs up puts on a pair of sunglasses and checks his watch. Jack Lovington pulls up in a taxi cab. Lenny Ringle gets in the back.)* What took you so long? I've been waiting for ten minutes.

JACK LOVINGTON. Sorry, sir.

LENNY RINGLE. Drive, driver.

JACK LOVINGTON. Yes, sir. Sorry, sir.

LENNY RINGLE. Make a right at the light.

JACK LOVINGTON. Yes, sir.

LENNY RINGLE. Yes, sir. Sorry, sir. Jesus, Lovington. A kick in the crotch every day, ain't it? *(He takes off his sunglasses.)*

JACK LOVINGTON. Mr. Ringle?

LENNY RINGLE. Yeah, kid. It's me. Been looking all over for ya. Where ya been? How come you're not skating for me anymore?

JACK LOVINGTON. I'm sorry, Mr. Ringle. I just had some ...

LENNY RINGLE. Cut the Mr. Ringle routine, it ain't even my real name. Just call me Lenny.

JACK LOVINGTON. Okay, Lenny.

LENNY RINGLE. So what? Pay not good enough? You can't tell me you're getting more at the cardboard factory or this lousy gig.

JACK LOVINGTON. It ain't that, Lenny. That night at the Armory was the greatest night of my life, that's the truth.

LENNY RINGLE. Then what's with the disappearing act, huh? I got 'em lined up around the block waiting for Gentleman Jack

Lovington.

JACK LOVINGTON. Aurora.

LENNY RINGLE. Got a girl, huh?

JACK LOVINGTON. *(Pointing to the dash.)* That's her right there. My fiancée.

LENNY RINGLE. Kinda homely. Can she skate?

JACK LOVINGTON. No. She don't like the derby much.

LENNY RINGLE. *(Outraged.)* She don't?!

JACK LOVINGTON. She says it ain't got no dignity. Says it's just a fad and she ain't marrying no man who got no future. So I'm doing my shifts here, picking up some overtime at the factory.

LENNY RINGLE. Yeah, right, go bust your hump for a few extra nickels. Maybe one day you got enough to buy yourself a coffin. You gotta dump her, kid!

JACK LOVINGTON. Oh, I can't do that.

LENNY RINGLE. What? You knock her up? I can have that taken care of.

JACK LOVINGTON. No, Lenny.

LENNY RINGLE. That's right, you're a catholic. 'Scuse me.

JACK LOVINGTON. No, I ain't got her pregnant. We got separate beds and everything. It's just we been engaged for two years now. And I love her.

LENNY RINGLE. You got loyalties, I respect that. But what are you doing to yourself, kid? Slaving at some factory just so you can get in a cab, drive a bunch know-nothings and never was's around and then come home to a woman who don't see the derby for the beautiful thing me and you know it to be?!

JACK LOVINGTON. My dad drove a cab and my mother worked at that cardboard factory. These are good jobs.

LENNY RINGLE. Yeah and where are your parents now?

JACK LOVINGTON. Well …

LENNY RINGLE. Dead, kid! Your mom got brown lung disease and your dad got run over by a rib truck. Spent the rest of your childhood at the orphanage. Make a right.

JACK LOVINGTON. How did you know that?

LENNY RINGLE. A right, kid.

JACK LOVINGTON. *(Turning right.)* Oh, okay.

LENNY RINGLE. Heard the whole two-hanky story from that shyster over at Saint Barbara's.

JACK LOVINGTON. How did you know what …

LENNY RINGLE. And donating half your salary to the church?!

Didn't know God was hurtin' that bad.

JACK LOVINGTON. The roof needs repairing. And Father Kosciusko's not a ... what did you call him?

LENNY RINGLE. A shyster.

JACK LOVINGTON. Yeah, well you take that back. Father practically raised me. He's a man of God.

LENNY RINGLE. Must be some hole in that roof, 'cause I roll out a five-spot and the good Father told me everything I needed to know and more

JACK LOVINGTON. ... That's a lie.

LENNY RINGLE. You a bed-wetter, Jack?

JACK LOVINGTON. I can't believe he told you that ...

LENNY RINGLE. Nah ... I'm just messing with you, kid. Your buddy Deepadova at the factory ratted you out.

JACK LOVINGTON. Oh.

LENNY RINGLE. I made the bed-wetting thing up.

JACK LOVINGTON. Oh.

LENNY RINGLE. We'll keep it between me and you.

JACK LOVINGTON. Okay look, you could say a lot of things, Lenny. But don't say nothing more about Father Kosciusko ...

LENNY RINGLE. I can see he means a lot to you.

JACK LOVINGTON. ... and nothing about God while you're in my cab. Okay? We're all here on God's time, Lenny. You may think that's dumb, but I know it's the truth.

LENNY RINGLE. Whatever you want to believe, kid. Me? I'm a business man. I believe in facts. I'll shut up about God but you hear me out on some facts. Fact. You're busting your hump, working two jobs that don't pay nothing. Fact. You're giving half of your nothing to that racketeer over at Saint Barbara's, the other half to some harpy, dog-faced girl who's got you jumping over fire hydrants because all she's giving you is the tit and not the steak.

JACK LOVINGTON. *(Takes out his rosary.)* Lenny!

LENNY RINGLE. Fact! You're the best damn skater I've seen in five years of running the roller derby! And fact, I can give you one hundred fifty dollars a week to ditch this two-bit life and come on tour with me and the New York Bombers!

JACK LOVINGTON. How much?

LENNY RINGLE. Make a right.

JACK LOVINGTON. *(Turning right.)* The New York Bombers?! With Charlie Heartbreak. Jerry Kiger, Cindy Gums?! They're my heroes.

LENNY RINGLE. That's right, the big time, kid! None of this Jersey City bridge and tunnel bupkis. A three-month barnstorming tour up and down the east coast.

JACK LOVINGTON. Three months, that's, that's …

LENNY RINGLE. Eighteen hundred bucks. Buy a whole new set of pews for the church, buy your girl a mink coat, maybe a car …

JACK LOVINGTON. I still got to get her an engagement ring.

LENNY RINGLE. Perfect. Get her a ring. And my guess is, with a face like that her parents didn't put a whole lot aside for a wedding.

JACK LOVINGTON. Huh?

LENNY RINGLE. You're gonna need the extra bread.

JACK LOVINGTON. Oh. Yeah.

LENNY RINGLE. We got a bus leaving Saturday night at eleven o'clock. Flatbush Station. Pull over here.

JACK LOVINGTON. Hey wait, this is where I picked you up. You ain't gone nowhere.

LENNY RINGLE. "Going" nowhere, kid. Sound like somebody's life, you know? *(He hands him some cash and gets out of the cab.)*

JACK LOVINGTON. Ten dollars!

LENNY RINGLE. This so-called life you got here? It's just going in circles. Going nowhere. But, Jack, there's another place where going in circles gets you somewhere. Somewhere big! And that place is the derby! And it needs you. *(He starts walking away.)*

JACK LOVINGTON. Wait, you got change coming to you, Lenny.

LENNY RINGLE. Give it to me on the bus, kid. Eleven P.M. Flatbush Station. *(Lights down on Lenny and Jack. Lights up on Al Deepadova, Jack's Neanderthal boss at the factory, reading a letter with a perplexed look on his face.)*

AL DEEPADOVA. Dear Mr. Deepadova. There are many beautiful things in flight and so little time to catch them. If I had time enough in a mason jar, believe me, I would stay in Brooklyn until I was still and forgotten. But like some strange wind that could not move porch chimes but managed to tear a hole through the earth, I have quietly reclaimed my life. From the kindest part of my heart, please except this letter of resignation with the same grace that follows you in all your endeavors. Your factory has been a warm, warm place. Alas, it was not for me. *(Lights down on Al Deepadova. Lights up on Bennie, Jack's cigar-chomping dispatcher.)*

BENNIE, THE DISPATCHER. Dear Bennie. Although my efforts at friendship have been met with pristine disdain, there remains a place reserved for you at my table. I read in the *Catholic Worker* last week something I cannot shake out of my bones. We do not deny the Provider. Driving through the blushing black night of the city, a wolf at every corner it seemed, your voice delivered me one moment closer to the sleep I so desperately needed. Bennie, for reasons larger than myself, I can no longer drive a cab for you. You've been the best of myrrhbearers. *(Lights down on Bennie, the Dispatcher. Lights up on Mrs. Yojimbo, the weird and cranky green grocer.)*

MRS. YOJIMBO. Dear Mrs. Yojimbo. So many drab days and so much dreary weather, it seemed I almost lost myself, my most profound and private thoughts shattered against this familiar plot of concrete. On days like these, I found myself suddenly upon your corner store. *(Lights up on Jack Lovington in his apartment writing a letter on powder blue stationery. He sits at a desk, a packed suitcase sits by the door.)* And among the assaulting plums and fungi, the noodle soups and yellow-red bananas, I found my footing, and sense of wonder returned to me. Mrs. Yojimbo, I am leaving our neighborhood for a while but not before I thought to leave you this brief note of thanks. Your bok choy was so cold, so delicious. Jack Lovington ... Who's Jack Lovington? *(Lights down on Mrs. Yojimbo. Lights up on Father Kosciusko, reading a letter. We hear the sound of drips in a bucket.)*

FATHER KOSCIUSKO. Dear Father Kosciusko. I woke up this morning before the sun did. I walked around our neighborhood and swapped gossip with the ghosts of my upbringing. This morning, it felt like all the cosmic dust Our Father in Heaven saves for the planets and the stars fell on Bushwick. And as I slipped inside to say the holy rosary among Saint Barbara's pillared dark, I knew I didn't have the fortitude to tell you what I'm telling you now. *(Father Kosciusko starts skimming the letter. Jack puts down his pen gets on his knees to pray.)*

JACK LOVINGTON. Lord, make me an instrument of thy peace. And where there is hatred, let me so love. Where there is injury, pardon. Where there is doubt, faith. Where there is despair, hope.

FATHER KOSCIUSKO. Oh no no no NO NO. *(Father Kosciusko grabs a coat and runs offstage. The drip sound fades.)*

JACK LOVINGTON. Where there is darkness, light. *(There is a knock at Jack's front door.)*

JACK LOVINGTON. Ah nuts. I'M PRAYING IN HERE!

FATHER KOSCIUSKO. *(Offstage.)* Open the door!

JACK LOVINGTON. Father? *(Jack gets up, opens the door for Father Kosciusko, who is brandishing a letter.)*

FATHER KOSCIUSKO. What in God's name is this all about, Jack Lovington?!

JACK LOVINGTON. I knew you were gonna be upset.

FATHER KOSCIUSKO. A cowardly act, Jack. Cowards do this.

JACK LOVINGTON. Maybe.

FATHER KOSCIUSKO. Why didn't you come and talk to me, face to face?

JACK LOVINGTON. I don't know. I just got all these things to say and they don't never sound good when I tries to talk 'em outta my mouth. So's I write 'em down.

FATHER KOSCIUSKO. You wrote this yourself?

JACK LOVINGTON. Yeah.

FATHER KOSCIUSKO. Well, they're lovely words, Jack. Beautiful sentiments. Unquestionably the product of a proper Catholic education. But, the ROLLER DERBY, Jack?! Really now, aren't we taking this too far?

JACK LOVINGTON. It's only for three months. I'll send money for the orphans back every week …

FATHER KOSCIUSKO. I'm worried about your soul, not your money, Jack! I should've forbade you when I had the chance.

JACK LOVINGTON. *(Passionately.)* How come God gave me this roller skatin' gift and then makes me gotta work in a cardboard factory and drive a cab?! Tell me, Father?! What kind of God is that?!

FATHER KOSCIUSKO. Do not bring God into this! Believe me, God has more pressing issues to deal with than one man's self-serving delusions. Really, the arrogance.

JACK LOVINGTON. Thanks for the advice, Father. *(He goes to his writing desk, continues writing on the powder blue stationery.)*

FATHER KOSCIUSKO. Don't you turn your back on me, son!

JACK LOVINGTON. I'm not a kid in the orphanage anymore, Father! You can't tell me what to do!

FATHER KOSCIUSKO. It's this Lenny person, isn't it? He's the one corrupting you, isn't he?

JACK LOVINGTON. I got my own brain. I got my reasonings.

FATHER KOSCIUSKO. I met him, you know. This man you're going to run out on Aurora for. A very sinister figure, Jack.

JACK LOVINGTON. I'm not running out on Aurora, and no offense or nothing, Father, but I'm beginning to think you think everything's sinister. *(He begins to fold and seal the powder blue letter.)*

FATHER KOSCIUSKO. If your parents in heaven could see you now … so lost.

JACK LOVINGTON. I tried to tell Aurora it's only three months, she don't wanna hear nothing! She says you go with them, Jack Lovington, then it's over between us, and then she slams the door and runs out to her mother's, I think.

FATHER KOSCIUSKO. Well, she's in pain, Jack! Aurora's in pain. She feels pushed aside for a pair of roller skates.

JACK LOVINGTON. I don't want her to feel that way. I try and tell her I'm doing this for us, she thinks I'm trying to get out of marrying her. I says I'm doing this so we *can* get married! So's I can love her the way she wants to be loved, but I don't know, everything comes out Swanee river. I talk like a caveman!

FATHER KOSCIUSKO. You have to see it from her eyes, Jack. You haven't even got her a ring yet, she's still got insecurities. I mean first off, she's not an attractive woman …

JACK LOVINGTON. Yes, she is. How come people are always saying that?!

FATHER KOSCIUSKO. She's got a beautiful inside.

JACK LOVINGTON. No, she's got a beautiful face, too! Geez. She's always been beautiful. It's just she just don't got no sense of the world outside of Brooklyn. She don't even got no curiosity about it. It's suffocating.

FATHER KOSCIUSKO. And what do you know about it, Jack? Hmm, Mr. World Traveler? What you do know beyond the, how do you put it … *(He refers to Jack's letter.)* … the cosmic dust that falls on Bushwick?

JACK LOVINGTON. I know something's out there for me.

FATHER KOSCIUSKO. I've seen a little bit of the world, Jack. You might not be ready for what's out there. There are things out there you won't find on your way to and from the factory. Rock 'n' roll. Hot roadsters. Drive-in movies.

JACK LOVINGTON. So?

FATHER KOSCIUSKO. People drive their cars, SIT in their cars and watch movies. It's true! "Murphy" beds. "Bus" depots, burger "joints."

JACK LOVINGTON. *(A little scared.)* I know about those things.

FATHER KOSCIUSKO. Do you?

JACK LOVINGTON. Some of them. But it don't matter none, 'cause I'm going stay in my hotel room and read my Bible when I'm not skating. And I'll come back with enough money for a wedding and we can do the "I do's" in front of you and the whole congregation and have a real good honeymoon.

FATHER KOSCIUSKO. I hope she'll still have you when get back. *(Jack holds up the powder blue letter.)*
JACK LOVINGTON. She reads this letter, she will. I poured an ocean in it, everything inside of me. *(He checks his watch.)* What time you got, Father? *(Father Kosciusko checks his pocket watch.)*
FATHER KOSCIUSKO. Ten-thirty.
JACK LOVINGTON. Me too. Oh geez, I'm gonna be late. *(He double-checks his suitcase. While he tidies up ...)* Alright, look, Father, could you wait here for Aurora until she comes back. She's awful mad at me and you always know what's right to say.
FATHER KOSCIUSKO. I suppose I could.
JACK LOVINGTON. Oh and yeah, here's some money for Aurora. It's everything I got, all except ten bucks, and could you make sure she gets this too? It's on powder blue paper. Powder blue that's her favorite color. *(He hands him the money and a powder blue envelope.)*
FATHER KOSCIUSKO. Sure.
JACK LOVINGTON. And when Aurora gets back, could you tell her I'm sorry and that I'll call her every chance I get.
FATHER KOSCIUSKO. I'll tell her that, Jack.
JACK LOVINGTON. And I'll call you too, Father. And just in case she don't come back or you wanna go out and get a snack or something, here are the keys. The big key's for the outside. And the little key is for this door and ... *(He runs and hugs Father Kosciusko.)*
FATHER KOSCIUSKO. Alright, Jack. This is awkward. *(Lights down. Lights up on Flatbush Station, a chartered bus with its motor going. A group of assembled skaters sit in different rows. Charlie Heartbreak, an intimdating guy who rarely looks up from his crossword puzzle; "Specs" Macedo, a tough guy with Coke bottle glasses; Cindy Gums, a bubble-gum-chewing Japanese girl. Other skaters, male and female, are cut-outs. Lenny Ringle stands in the stairwell of the bus looking out the door. A female bus driver from Illinois waits at the wheel.)*
FEMALE BUS DRIVER. It's 11:10. Might wanna get going ...
LENNY RINGLE. Not much longer. *(Jerry "Three Nuts" Kiger boards the bus. Lenny hands him an envelope.)* You're late, Jerry.
JERRY KIGER. I got here, didn't I?
LENNY RINGLE. Lucky me. *(Jerry takes a seat in the back.)*
FEMALE BUS DRIVER. Okay now, you only got three hours charter time to get to Connecticut. Can't start breaking speed laws now.
LENNY RINGLE. Just gimme another minute, will ya?
SPECS MACEDO. Lenny, man, who we waiting for?
LENNY RINGLE. Maybe nothing.

FEMALE BUS DRIVER. Fifty miles an hour, that's as fast as the law lets me.

LENNY RINGLE. Yeah, I heard ya.

CHARLIE HEARTBREAK. Maybe who you waiting for ain't coming.

LENNY RINGLE. Maybe you're right, Charlie. Alright, driver, let's get this rig rolling. We're making a stop right before the BQE.

FEMALE BUS DRIVER. Get out of the stairwell, Mister, and I'll make any stop you want. *(Lenny Ringle steps out of the stairwell.)*

JACK LOVINGTON. *(Offstage.)* Wait! Wait! Hold that bus!

FEMALE BUS DRIVER. Heading out. *(The Female Bus Driver closes the door and hits the gas as Jack Lovington leaps onto the bus.)*

JACK LOVINGTON. Hey Lenny! *(Lenny hands Jack an envelope.)*

LENNY RINGLE. Thought you gave up on us, kid.

JACK LOVINGTON. You can't give up on a dream, Lenny! Hi everyone. I'm a big fan of all of youse. *(Jack goes to take a seat.)*

LENNY RINGLE. Ain't you forgetting something?

JACK LOVINGTON. Oh yeah. Thanks again for believing in me, Lenny.

LENNY RINGLE. No. I got some change coming to me. From the cab ride.

JACK LOVINGTON. Oh, right. I forgot.

LENNY RINGLE. Kid thinks I'm made of money.

JERRY KIGER. A regular Rockefeller!

CHARLIE HEARTBREAK. Born on the corner of "three dollar bill" and "whose dime is this."

LENNY RINGLE. That's enough out of you guys.

JACK LOVINGTON. All's I got is a ten. *(Lenny takes the ten, pockets it.)*

LENNY RINGLE. That'll do. Family, this is Jack. He's A-1 on the skates but a little green, so don't hose him too bad. Kid, this is your new family. Eduardo "Specs" Macedo.

SPECS MACEDO. Whatcha looking at?

LENNY RINGLE. Cindy Gums.

CINDY GUMS. *(Almost threatening.)* You got a girlfriend?

JACK LOVINGTON. I'm engaged. *(Charlie, Jerry and Specs start laughing.)* What's so funny?

CHARLIE HEARTBREAK. Charlie says good luck.

LENNY RINGLE. Jerry "Three Nuts" Kiger. Carol "Big Tickets" Moreland. Carol likes to wear her uniform. Isn't that right, Carol? And this here's Charlie Heartbreak.

JACK LOVINGTON. Charlie Heartbreak, the best blocker I ever seen.

CHARLIE HEARTBREAK. Charlie don't shake hands.

LENNY RINGLE. Take a seat kid. Driver, remind me when we're by the BQE.

FEMALE BUS DRIVER. You betcha.

LENNY RINGLE. Now family, I want to thank you all for your commitment to me and to the derby. *(Jerry looks in his envelope.)*

JERRY KIGER. Is this all we're getting paid?

LENNY RINGLE. That's for food, Kiger! First things first, the whatsit and whosit, so pay attention! Now most of you know each other, know you're the best in the business (at least in the New York area, which is a bit dried up at the moment), so I had an idea and the TV suits agreed, so this is why we're going on the road. You're on this bus which is going to, where are we going again, driver?

FEMALE BUS DRIVER. Hartford.

LENNY RINGLE. Hartford, right. And at Hartford we're going to meet up with the New England circuit and form a barnstorming tour. Now this bus is gonna be the Bombers and the Chicago Four-Wheelers. There's a bus going to Philadelphia got brand new teams, the Los Angeles Stranglers and the Midwest Pioneers. Your partner assignments are inside your envelope.

CINDY GUMS. *(Looking in her envelope.)* I got you, Specs.

CHARLIE HEARTBREAK. *(Looking in his envelope.)* Charlie got Carol "Big Tickets."

SPECS MACEDO. Lenny?

LENNY RINGLE. Yeah, Specs.

SPECS MACEDO. Ain't the L.A. Stranglers insensitive to the victims of the L.A. Strangler?

LENNY RINGLE. What do you mean?

"SPECS" MACEDO. He killed those people with his bare hands. I got family in L.A.

LENNY RINGLE. Too late, I already ordered the uniforms.

JERRY KIGER. And Lenny?

LENNY RINGLE. What is it, Jerry?

JERRY KIGER. How come you got a team from Chicago and one from the Midwest? Ain't Chicago in the Midwest?

LENNY RINGLE. Your point is?

FEMALE BUS DRIVER. I think he's trying to say, what if you're from Champaign, Illinois? Like I'm from. Most of the time we in Champaign like to root for the Bears in football, but now you give us two derby teams near us, we get confused.

CINDY GUMS. I'd be confused.

CHARLIE HEARTBREAK. Who Charlie supposed to root for if he's from Champaigne?

LENNY RINGLE. I don't think the Champaigne, Illinois, market's gonna make or break us.

CINDY GUMS. What if you're from Texas and you got no team?

SPECS MACEDO. Or Puerto Rico?

JERRY KIGER. Geographically, this don't make much sense.

CINDY GUMS. What if it was the Puerto Rico Stranglers and Los Angeles Pioneers?

SPECS MACEDO. I got family in Puerto Rico.

LENNY RINGLE. Could everyone shut up for a second?! Jesus. Alright, it don't matter where the team comes from, 'cause the whole point is that nobody's supposed to care about them. It's all about the Bombers, see? Every town we go into we want the Bombers to be the home team. We got great ratings in New York but nowhere else, and we got to do something about that or the derby's through. So, we ain't never going to no Texas or San Juan or Champaigne, Illinois, but …

JERRY KIGER. We want them to watch us on the TV, right?

CHARLIE HEARTBREAK. That's smart. Real smart.

LENNY RINGLE. Damn right it's smart! And three months from now, when all you brainiacs are skating in Madison Square Garden for the Roller Derby Championship, everybody and his mother with a TV set is gonna be rooting for the New York Bombers!

CINDY GUMS. We're going skate at the Garden?!

LENNY RINGLE. That's right, zipperpuss. So here's the skinny — the Bombers win everywhere they go, and any of you is on any team I tell you to be on each night. Everyone except for Charlie Heartbreak and Jack. You're both on the Bombers permanently.

SPECS MACEDO. How come the rookie gets to be on the Bombers?

LENNY RINGLE. 'Cause the kid ain't wearing Coke-bottle glasses and taking a Brodie every night, and 'cause he's got a fresh face and he don't ask questions.

JACK LOVINGTON. What do you mean the Bombers win everywhere …

LENNY RINGLE. Shut up, kid.

JACK LOVINGTON. Okay.

FEMALE BUS DRIVER. We're coming up to the BQE.

LENNY RINGLE. Good! *(He looks out the window. Jack looks inside his envelope.)*

JACK LOVINGTON. *(To Charlie.)* Who's Lindy Batello?

CHARLIE HEARTBREAK. What?

LENNY RINGLE. *(To the bus driver.)* Yeah, that's her by the hospital. The brunette with all the bags.

CHARLIE HEARTBREAK. Business man?

LENNY RINGLE. Skater man?

CHARLIE HEARTBREAK. What's a five-letter word for "keep this bus moving"?

LENNY RINGLE. I don't know. But I got a seven-letter word for "I run the business, you do your crossword."

CHARLIE HEARTBREAK. More trouble than she's worth, if you ask me.

LENNY RINGLE. Desperate times demand desperate action, but you're right. I didn't ask you. *(He gets off the bus. Offstage:)* Hey there, sunshine. *(Jack Lovington leans over the seat to Charlie Heartbreak.)*

JACK LOVINGTON. Who's getting on?

CHARLIE HEARTBREAK. Don't make eye contact, kid.

JACK LOVINGTON. Don't make …

CHARLIE HEARTBREAK. Charlie says don't look her in the eye and don't say nothing to her. *(Lindy Batello enters, wearing a hospital gown, carrying an almost finished bottle of rotgut. Lenny reenters with some suitcases.)*

LINDY BATELLO. Hurry up, doctors don't know I've left.

LENNY RINGLE. Packed a lot of stuff, Lindy.

LINDY BATELLO. What kind of fucking dump shit bus is this?

FEMALE BUS DRIVER. Oh, you're not talking about this bus, are ya?

LINDY BATELLO. Yeah, it's a fucking dump, ya dyke.

LENNY RINGLE. *(To bus driver.)* Sorry, she hasn't taken her pills yet.

LINDY BATELLO. You promised me something nice, Lenny. You said it was going to be first class this time, Lenny.

LENNY RINGLE. We're getting a new bus in Hartford. Family, you all know Lindy Batello. Lindy, I'm sure you know most of the men …

LINDY BATELLO. What's that supposed to mean?

LENNY RINGLE. Kid, how about helping me here? … Driver …

FEMALE BUS DRIVER. I'm not very happy.

LINDY BATELLO. Jerry, Specs … Charlie. *(Charlie Heartbreak looks up from his crossword, grunts, then returns to it. The bus pulls out. Jack grabs a few of Lindy's bags. Lindy sits in Jack's seat.)* Hey, be careful with my fucking bags, they got all my valuables and keepsakes in 'em.

JACK LOVINGTON. Yes, Ma'am.

LINDY BATELLO. If anything breaks in there I ain't gonna be so nice.

JACK LOVINGTON. Okay, sorry. *(She looks at him, Jack squeezes by her.)*

LINDY BATELLO. Is he a faggot?

JACK LOVINGTON. Huh?

LINDY BATELLO. *(To Jack.)* You like getting fucked in the trap door?

LENNY RINGLE. Lindy, leave him alone, the kid's your new partner. *(She looks him over.)*

LINDY BATELLO. Yeah? Well, Howdy-Doody better have a functional ten-inch dick like Three Nuts over there, or I can tell you right now, this is gonna get fucking boring, Lenny!

CHARLIE HEARTBREAK. Lord help us.

LINDY BATELLO. What's with the Jap girl?

LENNY RINGLE. Lindy!

CINDY GUMS. I'll tear your motherfucking heart out!

LINDY BATELLO. I like her. *(She looks over at Jack.)*

JACK LOVINGTON. Hi. I'm Jack. *(Lindy vomits into Jack's lap.)*

LINDY BATELLO. *(To Jack.)* Don't worry, it's mostly water. *(Lights out. We hear a choir, the end of a Catholic mass in Spanish. Lights up on Father Domingo at the pulpit, speaking into a microphone. Father Kosciusko is in his office, listening to the service on a speaker.)*

FATHER DOMINGO. *Oremos. Cierren sus ojos. Cierren sus ojos. Manden sus pensamentos al cielo. Cierren sus ojos. (Father Domingo closes his eyes, puts his hands together.) Virgen del Guadelupe, mira nos con gracia, Madre Santisima, en este pueblo chiquito de Bushwick. Sabemos que tienes muchos hijos y sabemos que oyes muchas oraciones en varios pueblo y no estamos pidiendo un gran milagro. Somos tus hijos, Madre Santisima. Venimos de Puerto Rico, de Mexico, El Salvador, Panama, venimos del todo el mundo. Caras a solliadas en las calles frias de Brooklyn. Somos tus ovejas perdidas, Madre Santisima, y pedimos por nada solamente comida y tu amor. Oremos. Mandanos un angel. (Father Domingo opens one eye, sees all are bent in prayer. He looks up and then moves his hands in circles. We hear the sound of pigeon wings flapping. A few gasps, some muttering from the pews. Father Kosciusko shakes his head, starts writing a letter.) Si. Si. Si. Te oremos y te oremos siempre. Por tu gracia, por tu amor, por estos dias preciosos que tenemos vos nosotros. Madre Santisima, nunca apares tu mivada te nosotros. (Father Domingo holds out his arms. Much fluttering of wings, then a row of cut-out pigeons appears on the outstretched arms of Father Domingo.) Amen. (The congregation repeats "amen." We hear some awed Spanish voices and then applause. Father Domingo smiles. Father Kosciusko, turns off the speaker. Father Koscuisko looks at his letter.)*

FATHER KOSCIUIKO. *(Reading.)* Dear Archbishop McCullough. I am compelled to write to you concerning the unorthodox methods of your new appointee, Father Domingo. Admittedly, I was hesitant to acknowledge the "demographic" changes that have come to pass in our parish and though I have nothing personally against the Spanish language or the speakers of it, the kind of "showmanship" that accompanies the current seven o'clock service would shame even the most progressive factions of the church. I implore you to … *(A phone rings.)* Of course. *(The phone rings again. He answers it.)* Hello, Saint Barbara's? *(Lights up on Jack Lovington at a pay phone, in his Bombers uniform. We hear sounds from an unruly arena crowd and some dank rock 'n' roll.)*

JACK LOVINGTON. *(Talking loud.)* Hey Father. It's Jack Lovington.

FATHER KOSCIUSKO. Jack? Jack! I'm right in the middle of seven o'clock mass. *(Suddenly Lindy Batello, wearing a Bombers jersey, knocks Father Domingo offstage. His birds scatter. One flies into Father Kosciusko's office, unseen.)*

JACK LOVINGTON. I'm sorry, Father.

FATHER KOSCIUSKO. Not that I have any idea what they're saying. Where are you? How come you weren't at morning services today?

JACK LOVINGTON. I'm in Pittsburgh.

FATHER KOSCIUSKO. You haven't been to services for three weeks. What's that noise in the background? Why are you shouting?

JACK LOVINGTON. That's the crowd. They got almost eight hundred people here. I'm traveling with the derby, Father, remember?

FATHER KOSCIUSKO. Oh, yes. Right. Well, how it that going?

JACK LOVINGTON. It's mostly great, Father. You won't believe it. I already been to Bridgeport and Albany and Syracuse! It's beautiful out here. Oh, the derby's not everything I thought it was. My team keeps winning all the time, something ain't right about it.

FATHER KOSCIUSKO. Are you staying out of trouble?

JACK LOVINGTON. Oh, sure. Of course, the team's always trying to get me to go out with them … crazy bunch of guys. They tease me. Ya know, spit on the rookie. Kick the rookie in the stomach. Give the rookie the one-eyed Roscoe.

FATHER KOSCIUSKO. What's the one-eyed Roscoe?

JACK LOVINGTON. *(Pause, a painful memory.)* It's not a nice thing, Father. I'm gonna be okay … uh, how are the orphans, how's the neighborhood?

FATHER KOSCIUSKO. Bushwick's changing, Jack. Our people don't come like they used to. Oh, the others come. Come for Father Domingo's bird extravaganza, and they're pleasant enough, I guess, with their holas and buenos dias. But I know what's happening. He's pushing me out.

JACK LOVINGTON. Nah, Father Domingo's a good guy, Father. He wouldn't do that.

FATHER KOSCIUSKO. I feel like the third donkey in line for the ark. You know what I mean? You ever feel that way, Jack?

JACK LOVINGTON. Like a donkey? *(Father Kosciusko sees the cut-out pigeon in his office.)*

FATHER KOSCIUSKO. Could you hold on, Jack? *(Father Kosciusko chases the bird out of his office with the phone. The entire men's Bomber team [cut-outs, too] enters the stage, they watch with horror from the pit as Bert Fineberg describes the action with "Larry Calloway" and his microphone.)*

BERT FINEBERG. And a clean game's been put on hold here in the third period as Lindy Batello, brought out of semi-retirement, has brought her A game here to Pittsburgh. A as in all fists, all the time. *(We hear the crowd begin to boo.)* A vicious uppercut to Beth Nutterman, unseen by the referee, who's either blind in the eye or fat on the Batello payola.

JACK LOVINGTON. I'm still here, Father. Yeah, I was wondering if you seen Aurora? 'Cause she don't seem to be home when I call.

BERT FINEBERG. A kick to the breadbasket and a chop to the throat, and down goes Cindy Gums.

JACK LOVINGTON. She gave you a letter? How come she didn't mail it herself, I left her the address? Well, could you send it to me? Thanks.

BERT FINEBERG. Another senseless roundhouse from Batello, leaving the Lady Strangler with a smile only a dentist could love.

JACK LOVINGTON. She come to mass with who? Al Deepadova?!

BERT FINEBERG. Holy crow! The brunette bomber rakes the eyeballs of Carol Moreland.

JACK LOVINGTON. They took communion together? Holding hands? Ah Christ! Sorry Father.

BERT FINEBERG. That may or may not be nail polish on Batello's fingers, folks.

JACK LOVINGTON. Right now? Holy Mary mother of god pray for us sinners now and at the hour of our death, amen. *(We hear more angry jeers from the crowd, beer cans are thrown at the men in the pit. One by one they begin to leave the stage.)*

BERT FINEBERG. The crowd's beginning to show some of that legendary Pittsburgh pugnacity.

JACK LOVINGTON. Al Deepadova? Are you sure, Father? The last three weeks?

BERT FINEBERG. That three-rivers ruggedness that makes this the steel capital of the country. I think the shell of my Chevy Tornado was made right here in this gritty city. A great car!

JACK LOVINGTON. Oh no. NO! I don't got no more change, operator.

BERT FINEBERG. And here comes Cindy Gums, drawing blood, biting Batello in the arm, showing us why she got that nickname in the first place. Children, now might be a great time to double check that arithmetic homework.

JACK LOVINGTON. Look inside myself? I'm not the one holding hands with Al Deepadova, am I? *(Riots sounds begin. Bert ducking a Bluto Beer. Charlie runs past Jack.)*

CHARLIE HEARTBREAK. Charlie says run. They gonna riot.

JACK LOVINGTON. Father, you still there? *(Specs Macedo runs past Jack.)* Father? *(Jerry "Three Nuts" runs past Jack.)* What's going on? *(Beth Nutterman runs past Jack.)*

BETH NUTTERMAN. Lindy forgot to take her pills.

BERT FINEBERG. We'll be right back with more roller derby thrills and spills. *(Cindy Gums runs past Jack with blood around her mouth, followed by Lindy holding her arm, screaming. Jack hangs up the phone.)*

JACK LOVINGTON. Aurora.

CHARLIE HEARTBREAK. *(Offstage.)* Start up the bus! Start up the bus!

BERT FINEBERG. Right after this word from Vacu-Vak. The vacuum that says, "Voila" to dirt! *(Lights down. Lights up on Lenny Ringle, who talks long enough to get everyone back in a locker room. Skaters for the Bombers and the Stranglers are getting ready for a new match.)*

LENNY RINGLE. Walt Disney lays out a map and says let's make us a Mickey Mouse theme park. FantasyLand, AdventureLand, you know. Buys the land, builds the rides, let's the people in. Only problem is they got some problems. They got a ride lets the kiddies drive a car. Kids don't know how to drive, drive all over the place smacking into the rails, running over the street sweepers. Blood all over Mickey. What's Walt gonna do? Blame it on the Elders of Zion? Hell no. He makes adjustments. He puts the cars on motorized tracks, kids can turn the wheel any way they want to. And now, no one dies in FutureLand. Mistakes happen. Hey you gotta move forward. So, that little scene two weeks ago in Pittsburgh? Thing of the past. Did I hear more than a few scenarios about what might happen to my person if something like Pittsburgh happened again on LIVE National TV? Sure. But who gives a crap about me? I'm just the visionary. Lindy!

LINDY BATELLO. What?

LENNY RINGLE. You know these pills them doctors gave you, the ones that kinda make you all happy?

LINDY BATELLO. You been going through my footlocker?

LENNY RINGLE. I want you to take one of these pills before each game.

LINDY BATELLO. Fuck yourself with a stick.

LENNY RINGLE. Okay, I got a better plan. You skate for the Stranglers tonight.

LINDY BATELLO. Stay out of my fucking locker, Lenny.

LENNY RINGLE. Nutterman, switch jerseys with Lindy, will ya?

BETH NUTTERMAN. Sure thing, boss.

LENNY RINGLE. Thank you. Cindy Gums?

CINDY GUMS. Yeah.

LENNY RINGLE. No more biting.

CINDY GUMS. No?

LENNY RINGLE. We don't bite in the derby.

CINDY GUMS. No bite?

LENNY RINGLE. Say it with me. I will not bite.

LENNY RINGLE and CINDY GUMS. I will not bite.

LENNY RINGLE. Great. You're golden. Take this just in case. *(He hands Cindy a mouth guard, then starts working the room.)* Alright now, new sponsor tonight, folks. Lonegan's Canned Meat. Meat in a can. You eat it all the time, so time never eats you. Got it?

ALL except LOVINGTON. Yeah.

LENNY RINGLE. Charlie!

CHARLIE HEARTBREAK. *(Lifeless.)* I eat it all the time. It's a favorite around my dinner table.

LENNY RINGLE. Cindy Gums!

CINDY GUMS. It's good food. Eat it!

LENNY RINGLE. That'll do. Jack!

JACK LOVINGTON. Huh?

LENNY RINGLE. Lonegan's meat?

JACK LOVINGTON. Excuse me?

LENNY RINGLE. I'm Bert. You're you. Hey, Jack, what do you think about Lonegan's Canned Meat?

JACK LOVINGTON. It's a great time to eat.

SPECS MACEDO. Rookie.

BETH NUTTERMAN. No, kid. It's like this. *(Lifeless.)* You eat it all the time, so the time never eats you.

JACK LOVINGTON. I eat it all the time, so it never eats me.

LENNY RINGLE. What's the matter, kid?

JACK LOVINGTON. I just got things on my mind.

SPECS MACEDO. Rookie's got lady problems back home.

JACK LOVINGTON. I been calling her like crazy the last two weeks, she don't never pick up. I gotta talk to her.

LENNY RINGLE. She's an outsider, kid. She don't know your heart. Reminds me, this came for you from your monsignor back home. *(Lenny hands Jack some mail. Jack looks through it.)* Now look, all of you. Tonight you gotta skate like the landlord's slipping you a note under the door.

JERRY KIGER. When don't we?

LENNY RINGLE. When do ya?

JERRY KIGER. Nuts to you.

LENNY RINGLE. Just for that, you get the pre-game interview with Fineberg. Take it to the curb.

JERRY KIGER. Ah, come on, Lenny.

LENNY RINGLE. Try me. *(Jerry exits. To Kiger:)* You got yourself a good, tough Rochester crowd out there, Kiger. *(Back to the locker room.)* Hell, half the Kodak factory skipped out on the wife's Salisbury steak to be here. But look, we got some TV suits up in the rafters, and they gotta see something other than Pittsburgh or they're gonna cancel the contract, and then it's back to the USO shows, Nutterman, and the aluminum siding, Specs.

CHARLIE HEARTBREAK. Charlie's getting paid, right, business man?

LENNY RINGLE. You going hungry, skater man? Has Lenny

Ringle ever left you hungry? Yeah, thought so. Stranglers! Lots of rough stuff tonight, but Lovington over there jams it home in the end, okay? NBC's got some bupkis studio drama about an ugly butcher lives with his mom. If we can't beat that we should all die of shame. *(Jack rips open a letter, looks inside.)* So all of you, C'MON! Let's help Rochester forget their miserable lives, whattaya say?!

ALL EXCEPT LOVINGTON. Alright!

JACK LOVINGTON. *(Distracted.)* Yeah.

LENNY RINGLE. Someone hit him. *(Jack pulls out pieces of powder blue paper, torn into shreds. Lights down. Lights up Bert Fineberg and Jerry Kiger. Jerry is wearing a Stranglers jersey and looking extremely stiff and nervous.)*

FIFTIES TV ANNOUNCER VOICE. It's time … for Roller Derby! America's fastest growing … most exciting sport! … Roller Derby! All the thrills and spills you've come to expect from your favorite television show, the Roller Derby! Sponsored by Lonegan's Canned Meat. The meat you eat all the time, so time never eats you! Lonegan's Canned Meat. The secret's out! Take it away, Bert Fineberg. *(Bert elbows Jerry, who snaps to attention.)*

BERT FINEBERG. Bert Fineberg here LIVE at the Rochester Civic Center, where tonight's match between the visiting Los Angeles Stranglers and your very own New York Bombers … We're joined here by Strangler blocker, Jerry "Three Nuts" Kiger. Jerry, what's the mood inside the Strangler locker room? *(We see the girls lined up, staring at each other, shoving for position. Lindy is wearing Strangler blue. Female cut-outs are held by the male members of the cast, dressed in black.)*

JERRY KIGER. Everyone knows my team's the best. I'm saying that without any modesty because it's true, Mr. Fineberg. The Four-Wheelers are number one.

BERT FINEBERG. You mean the Stranglers?

JERRY KIGER. What'd I say?

BERT FINEBERG. You said "the Four-Wheelers." That was the team you were on two weeks ago. *(The ref blows his whistle and the girls start skating, Lindy throwing elbows almost immediately.)*

JERRY KIGER. Well, you know Bert, I started the year with the Bombers, and then I got traded to the Pioneers. Now I've got my own team, the Four-Wheelers.

BERT FINEBERG. The Stranglers.

JERRY KIGER. Right, the Stranglers.

BERT FINEBERG. And there they are now, the Lady Stranglers,

up on the banked track. Aren't the ladies splendid tonight after a warm-up meal of Lonegan's Canned Meat?

JERRY KIGER. The meat we eat all the time.

BERT FINEBERG. And good for you, too. Now, Jerry, lotta colorful nicknames in Roller Derby, tell the good people at home why they call you "Three Nuts"?

JERRY KIGER. Well, Mr. Fineberg, I got one more part down there than most guys got.

BERT FINEBERG. OKAY, thank you Jerry Kiger. I see Batello and Nutterman breaking from the pack, and the referee's got his arms akimbo, and that means we're about to start another jam. Bombers five, Stranglers two. *(Lenny Ringle enters, mouthing some choice invectives to an exiting Jerry. He slips Bert Fineberg a slip of paper.)*

LINDY BATELLO. Get your freakin' hands off me.

BETH NUTTERMAN. Stop throwing the elbows then, honey. *(Lindy and Beth start skating in profile to the audience.)*

BERT FINEBERG. I've just been handed a note from the commish himself, Mr. Lenny Ringle

LINDY BATELLO. She's holding, ref! She's holding!

BERT FINEBERG. Says here, there's been a last minute trade. Batello to Los Angeles and Nutterman to the Bombers. *(Lindy hits Beth in the breast.)*

BETH NUTTERMAN. Owww. *(The ref whistles the jam dead. We hear boos from the crowd.)*

REFEREE. Penalty, open fist. Two minutes, number four, Los Angeles.

LINDY BATELLO. Go blow it out yer ass. *(The rest of the skaters catch up to Beth and Lindy.)*

BETH NUTTERMAN. Crazy bitch!

LINDY BATELLO. Fucking cunt muncher! *(Lenny enters and pulls Lindy from the track.)*

BERT FINEBERG. As the pack reforms, colorful language from L.A.'s newest red-shirt, Lindy Batello.

LINDY BATELLO. Who you calling red-shirt?

FAN FROM THE CROWD. Watch your mouth, Batello, I brought my family.

LINDY BATELLO. Yeah, you shoulda brought some paperbags then …

FAN FROM THE CROWD. Why I outta …

LINDY BATELLO. Save it for the 4-H Club, asshole.

BERT FINEBERG. Lindy, if I can have a second of your time, I'm sure some of our fans …

LINDY BATELLO. *(Looks into the camera.)* I eat canned meat all the time. It's better than eating that other crap.

BERT FINEBERG. Thank you, Lindy, but we're not going to commercial.

LINDY BATELLO. *(Annoyed.)* What do you want, Bert?

BERT FINEBERG. You and Beth Nutterman were really getting into it out there.

LINDY BATELLO. She's a cheat. She's grabbing me, she's holding me all the time, if you know what I mean.

BERT FINEBERG. Seems to be part of the Bombers strategy tonight, lots of delay tactics.

LINDY BATELLO. Excuse me, a second. *(Lindy takes off her skate and smashes Beth Nutterman in the face with it! The referee blows his whistle and ejects Lindy from the match. More boos, even louder. To the referee:)* Yeah, whatever. *(Back to the camera.)* Beth Nutterman is rat fink cheat and I don't mind telling everyone in this armpit of a building, what a louse she is. Beth Nutterman is a cheat and a queer, and the New York Bombers are a bunch of cheats, and everyone knows that Rochester is the biggest dump in all of everywhere. I'm glad I been traded.

FAN IN THE CROWD. Go back to Jersey, you fat Jersey cow.

BERT FINEBERG. That's enough, sir.

LINDY BATELLO. Flap your gums, flyboy, you're a loser! All a bunch losers! Every last one of you.

FAN IN THE CROWD. Batello's got a butt like Jell-O!

LINDY BATELLO. Proves you've been looking at it, no-cock. *(Lenny grabs the mike away from her.)*

BERT FINEBERG. And it's time to return to the track for more great Roller Derby action! The men are coming on to the track for the change over.

LINDY BATELLO. Did I do good, Lenny?

LENNY RINGLE. Not bad, Batello, they hate you, but it's a good hate. Oh, and you can't say cock on TV. *(We see the men come onstage, and the crowd suddenly starts cheering. Charlie and Jack strapping their helmets on side by side. Jack is holding the envelope with the ripped up blue love letter.)*

BERT FINEBERG. Listen to that crowd react, as the men Bombers take the track.

LINDY BATELLO. How about getting a burger after the game?

LENNY RINGLE. I got a date with Carol "Big Tickets."

LINDY BATELLO. Is that right?

LENNY RINGLE. Yep.

LINDY BATELLO. Fine.

BERT FINEBERG. Must be first sighting of roller derby's most popular duo. The decapitator and the captivator, Charlie Heartbreak and Gentleman Jack Lovington!

CHARLIE HEARTBREAK. Charlie says what's in the envelope?

JACK LOVINGTON. My powder blue heart.

LINDY BATELLO. Where did you find the kid?

LENNY RINGLE. Some porkchop from the cardboard factory. Whattaya think?

LINDY BATELLO. He's got a good five-stride.

LENNY RINGLE. Is that right?

JACK LOVINGTON. Tomorrow's supposed to be our six-and-a-half year anniversary. I think she might be cheatin'.

CHARLIE HEARTBREAK. Women can be cruel.

JACK LOVINGTON. Huh?

LINDY BATELLO. He got a girl?

LENNY RINGLE. He's engaged, but you know how I feel about outsiders. Messing with his head. Got him skating like a cigarette. Could be some extra bread in it for the right girl ...

LINDY BATELLO. Yeah? Is that right?

LENNY RINGLE. Maybe Cindy Gums likes him?

LINDY BATELLO. Yeah, well I got a thing for altar boys.

LENNY RINGLE. Didn't know that.

LINDY BATELLO. Yeah. Bring him around tonight. I could use the extra money. The owner's a cheap rat.

LENNY RINGLE. I'll tell him you said that. *(He exits, she follows him.)*

CHARLIE HEARTBREAK. You just put that letter away and follow Charlie Heartbreak and score them points, and afterwards I'll take you out for some beer and sluts.

JACK LOVINGTON. Yeah. Okay. *(Jack stuffs the envelope in his shorts and we hear the ref's whistle.)*

VOICE OF BERT FINEBERG. And the jam is on, Rochester! Larry Calloway with the play-by-play. *(Lights down. We hear the sound of drips in a bucket. Lights up on Father Domingo, sitting in the confessional. A bucket sits next to him. He is holding one of his pigeons. He listens to a woman wearing a wide-brimmed hat, in great distress. All we see of her lit is a pair of sensible shoes. They belong to Aurora.)*

VOICE OF AURORA. And we been engaged for over two years.

Two years Father. And he ain't even gotten me, no ring. My mother she said, what kind of man proposes with a gum wrapper? That ain't no real man. That ain't no man you can count on.

FATHER DOMINGO. Yes.

VOICE OF AURORA. She said two-year engagement? Who ever heard of such a thing? In my day you get married. The man goes off to war. You work in factory, make the bullets. He comes back with one arm. You don't say nothing about it.

FATHER DOMINGO. Yes.

VOICE OF AURORA. So I been patient, Father. More than patient. He said we don't got enough money for a big wedding. I said you're an orphan, you got no family, we don't need no big wedding.

FATHER DOMINGO. Oh.

VOICE OF AURORA. Yeah, I felt bad about saying that. And yeah, maybe I wasn't so nice about the jerk's stupid roller skating but he ain't never nice about me working at the flower shop. This is 1958. I'm a modern woman, Father. I wanna work. *(Father Domingo looks at the bucket.)*

FATHER DOMINGO. Yes.

VOICE OF AURORA. My mother said, he just wants you pregnant and watching the *Lucy* show. You should find yourself a man with one arm, like your father. They don't mind you working. You the one with two good arms. *(Father Domingo looks at his pigeon.)* So when Jack packed up that suitcase and left, left that letter with all them pretty words makes a girl wanna cry it's so pretty. Well, I don't know, Father, but I got so mad at the jerk. I'm sorry I'm saying jerk a lot, Father. But I got my limits. A modern girl's got her limits.

FATHER DOMINGO. Yes. *(Father Domingo puts the pigeon in the bucket, silencing the drip sound, but replacing it with put-upon pigeon cooing.)*

VOICE OF AURORA. So yeah, that night he left … I told him I was going to my mother's house. But I felt like a skunk, 'cause I wasn't at my mother's, I was at Al Deepadova's instead. *(Father Domingo puts one finger to his lips. The pigeon stops making noise.)*

FATHER DOMINGO. Oh yes.

VOICE OF AURORA. And so, look, I don't know but something happened that night, Father. Something 'tween me and Al Deepadova, alright. And I know, it's a sin. But when Jack left I told him it was over and that meant we wasn't engaged no more, right? So forgive me, Father, but I had feelings with Al Deepadova. I know I'm dirty and bad but I used the rhythm method and I'm

sure Jack loves me. I mean, Al. Al loves me. So please forgive me, Father. I feel good, but mostly I feel bad. *(She starts crying.)*
FATHER DOMINGO. Yes.
VOICE OF AURORA. Father Kosciusko?
FATHER DOMINGO. Domingo.
VOICE OF AURORA. Father Domingo? I thought you was the other Father.
FATHER DOMINGO. Yes.
VOICE OF AURORA. Could you go get Father Kosciusko?
FATHER DOMINGO. Domingo.
VOICE OF AURORA. Jesus Christ.
FATHER DOMINGO. *Jesus Christe. (She continues to cry.)* No, no, no. Shhhh. *(Father Domingo hands her a handkerchief through the confessional.)* It's okay.
VOICE OF AURORA. Thank you, Father. *(Lights down. Lights up on a motel room. we hear the sound of some 1950s orchestral pop from a radio.)*
JACK LOVINGTON. *(Offstage, slurring.)* Man's a wanderer. He wanders and he don't know where until he's got a woman in his life. *(After a moment we hear the sound of some cans being popped open. Offstage, slurring:)* She tells the Man what to do 'cause he wants her to, you know? And that's a beautiful thing, 'cause then they can love each other, ain't that right?
CHARLIE HEARTBREAK. *(Offstage.)* That's right. *(Charlie Heartbreak enters, holding up Jack, who is drinking from a paper bag. Jack is obliterated.)*
JACK LOVINGTON. *(Slurring.)* I love her.
CHARLIE HEARTBREAK. That's what you keep saying.
JACK LOVINGTON. I love her, Mrs. Yojimbo.
CHARLIE HEARTBREAK. Don't you throw up on me.
JACK LOVINGTON. *(Shouting.)* Auurrrrooorrrraaaa!
CHARLIE HEARTBREAK. Charlie don't like loud.
JACK LOVINGTON. *(Quietly.)* Auurrrooorrrraaaa! *(Charlie looks out over the audience. He points to the motel door.)*
CHARLIE HEARTBREAK. *(Calls out.)* Business man? *(We hear the sound of a car horn. Charlie gives the universal "a-okay" sign.)*
JACK LOVINGTON. Did you know something? Did you? I wrote her a love letter? The most beautiful love letter that Man ever wrote Woman, since the time of history. It's our anniversary.
CHARLIE HEARTBREAK. Shhhh. *(Charlie props Jack up against the door.)*

JACK LOVINGTON. I got lots of beautiful things in my heart. *(Charlie takes the paper bag from Jack's hand, then knocks on the door.)* VOICE OF LINDY BATELLO. Who is it? *(Charlie knocks again, then exits offstage.)* What's the fucking idea? *(She opens the door tying a skimpy bathrobe. Jack falls through the open door, hits his head.)* JACK LOVINGTON. Aurora? *(Lindy looks out over the audience. We hear a car horn.)*
LINDY BATELLO. Who's that? Oh. Don't forget my fucking money. *(She drags Jack through the motel door.)*
JACK LOVINGTON. I was just talking to Mrs. Yojimbo.
LINDY BATELLO. Ain't you the fucking berries?
JACK LOVINGTON. You're not Japanese.
LINDY BATELLO. You want some champagne?
JACK LOVINGTON. Champagne? With the little bubbles?
LINDY BATELLO. Yeah, I got a couple of cans at the quickie-mart. It's real good champagne.
JACK LOVINGTON. I ain't had no champagne tonight. I had a beer. And a whiskey. And three martinis. And some wine with fruit in it. Solomia. No, I mean. Sangria. That's it. It was a party. I broke open the piñata and there was lemon drops and licorice ropes and Father said I could have two 'cause I was an orphan and orphans are special.
LINDY BATELLO. Here. *(She gives him a glass of champagne. The vibrating bed stops vibrating.)*
JACK LOVINGTON. Little bubbles. *(Toasting.)* Happy anniversary. Wait. The bed's on the wrong side. This ain't my apartment. *(She drops her bathrobe, revealing a vintage Betty Paige corsety, knockout hubba hubba get up.)* Oh boy. Where's Aurora? *(She puts another quarter into the slot by the bed. the bed begins to vibrate. She walks over to him.)*
LINDY BATELLO. She ain't here. She went out to get some corn-flakes. *(She starts unzipping his pants. He tries to walk away, she walks with him.)*
JACK LOVINGTON. At Mrs. Yojimbo's? She closes at eight o'clock.
LINDY BATELLO. Tell me about her, Jack.
JACK LOVINGTON. Oh, she's a nice lady with the corner store. Good food.
LINDY BATELLO. About Aurora.
JACK LOVINGTON. Oh. Yeah. It's our sixth-and-a-half-year anniversary tonight. Okay.

LINDY BATELLO. Is she pretty, Jack?

JACK LOVINGTON. Yeah.

LINDY BATELLO. Prettier than me?

JACK LOVINGTON. Okay.

LINDY BATELLO. What's Howdy-Doody hiding in there? *(She pulls out an envelope. He grabs it back from her, falls on the bed, looks up at her.)*

JACK LOVINGTON. That's mine. It's special. Like an orphan. It's a snowstorm. I'm like Santa Claus.

LINDY BATELLO. You're fucking bombed.

JACK LOVINGTON. That's okay, Father, she don't know no better. *(To Lindy.)* No, you don't see. Look see. *(He opens the envelope, turns it upside down and shakes it. Out comes torn-up pieces of powder blue paper all over the bed.)* Snowflakes. Blue snow. Aurora?

LINDY BATELLO. It's Lindy.

JACK LOVINGTON. Aurora! *(She smacks him.)*

LINDY BATELLO. Lindy!

JACK LOVINGTON. Aurora! *(Lindy smacks him a couple of more times.)* OW! Alright. Thank you. Lindy.

LINDY BATELLO. Wake the fuck up, Howdy-Doody!

JACK LOVINGTON. You curse too much!

LINDY BATELLO. Is that right?!

JACK LOVINGTON. You talk like a sailor!

LINDY BATELLO. We gonna fuck or not?

JACK LOVINGTON. I gotta pee.

LINDY BATELLO. The can's over there.

JACK LOVINGTON. Thank you very much. *(Jack gets up and immediately falls on his face.)* Ow. *(Pause.)* Maybe I could pee here?

LINDY BATELLO. Yeah, take a shit.

JACK LOVINGTON. No, I can make it. I'll just leave my pants here. Watch my pants.

LINDY BATELLO. Yeah. *(He crawls offstage to the bathroom. Lindy goes to the ripped up blue paper. She looks at them. Begins to arrange the pieces together.)*

JACK LOVINGTON. *(Offstage.)* I gotta leave the door open or Aurora's gonna think I'm cheating on her with Sister Mary five fingers. Ha Ha Ha Ha, sorry Father … ha ha ha … *(He starts laughing. She finishes re-arranging. She reads it. It's astonishingly beautiful. She starts to cry. Lindy pours herself another glass of champagne, shaking her head. She opens her pill bottle, takes a few, washes them back with champagne. He stops laughing. Offstage:)* It's shaped like the bottom of a rocking horse. *(He starts laughing again. Offstage, laughing:)* It's my anniversary. Happy anniversary. *(He starts weeping. Horrible, phlegmy cries.)*

LINDY BATELLO. You okay, in there? Hey, Howdy-Doody? Hey. Hey. C'mon. Don't do that. Don't fucking cry in there. C'mon. It ain't that bad, you gotta fucking cry. We're gonna have fun, okay? C'mon. You're gonna get me sad. I fucking hate being sad. Please, don't do that.

JACK LOVINGTON. *(Offstage.)* I'm sorry.

LINDY BATELLO. Yeah, c'mon. Just stop it. It ain't no fucking good to cry. Nobody ever cares if you cry. They don't care nothing. *(We hear the sound of toilet flushing. She downs her champagne and messes up the letter again. He walks out.)* Alright that's good. Just come out. Yeah. *(He stumbles over to the bed. Sits down next to the ripped-up letter. He looks at it.)* Good, just sit down. *(He's about to cry again.)* Don't you fucking start …

JACK LOVINGTON. I'm sorry. I won't. I'm okay.

LINDY BATELLO. Jesus. She dump you or something?

JACK LOVINGTON. You wanna see her picture?

LINDY BATELLO. Sure, I guess.

JACK LOVINGTON. Could you hand me my pants?

LINDY BATELLO. *(Laughs.)* Here. *(He takes out his wallet.)* You like this music? *(He hands her Aurora's picture. Lindy has the universal reaction to a picture of Aurora.)*

JACK LOVINGTON. Aurora. Ain't she pretty?

LINDY BATELLO. Yeah.

JACK LOVINGTON. I met her when I was no bigger than a sweater dog. She was so good and round. Like a dodge ball but more girly-like. All the kids at high school called me orphan boy, or dipstick, or orphan dipstick. But she called me Jackie. She was nice to me. She used to share me a baloney sandwich when I didn't have nothing. She likes cold cuts. That's her favorite. She also likes them wasabi peas at Mrs. Yojimbo's. That's her second favorite. I wrote her this love letter on powder blue paper 'cause she was so upset with me going on the derby tour. We supposed to be engaged except I didn't get her no ring.

LINDY BATELLO. Only one guy ever written me a love letter.

JACK LOVINGTON. You want another one? I could piece it back to together. *(He starts piecing it back together.)*

LINDY BATELLO. This dumb fucking kid named Reginal.

JACK LOVINGTON. It's a real good one.

LINDY BATELLO. Black guy. A real sweet talker.

JACK LOVINGTON. Lots of good, pretty words I think up in my head.

LINDY BATELLO. Fucking great kisser.

JACK LOVINGTON. I'll just cross out my name and put in Re-gin-nal. And then I'll cross out Aurora's name and put your name on it. What's your name again? *(She kisses him.)*

LINDY BATELLO. Aurora.

JACK LOVINGTON. Huh?

LINDY BATELLO. Aurora.

JACK LOVINGTON. *(Pause.)* Oh. Aurora.

LINDY BATELLO. Yeah. *(She kisses him again.)*

JACK LOVINGTON. We was waiting until we got married.

LINDY BATELLO. You don't have to wait no more.

JACK LOVINGTON. I love you, Aurora.

LINDY BATELLO. I love you, too.

JACK LOVINGTON. Happy anniversary, Aurora.

LINDY BATELLO. Yeah, shut the fuck up. *(She gets on top of him and turns off the light. Lights up on Father Kosciusko, who pulls out ten dollars from an envelope, sets it aside and reads a letter from Jack.)*

FATHER KOSCIUSKO. Dear Father. Springfield, Phoenixville, Silver Spring, Richmond. The towns keep changing but what I see of them doesn't. The arenas are loud and then they are dark. The diners never close and the motels all look the same, but what happens inside them cannot be duplicated. That is to say, if you're open to miracles and the stars are aligned, the weakest soup can be a feast, the humblest roof sheltering the best of rooms. A week ago, in what seemed my darkest hour, my very bones hollowed out by betrayal, God sent me an angel. And this Angel stared into my eyes and called the broken parts of me forward — my shattered spirit blown back into spun glass, my withered hands made whole again. I cannot say I trust this unrecognizable face in the mirror. I do not know if this too-soon recovery has flooded my body with false forgiveness and surrender. All I know is this. I am unbearably in love. And the world is water, strange to the touch. Jack Lovington. *(Lights up on a nurse holding a blue bag, and Lenny Ringle. Jack enters, wearing his Bombers jersey and holding a cup of his own urine.)*

JACK LOVINGTON. It hurts real bad when I pee.

NURSE. I need that.

JACK LOVINGTON. Yes, Ma'am.

FATHER KOSCIUSKO. P.S. I still dream of Aurora. Am I a bad

person? *(Music fades. Father Kosciusko exits. The nurse exits with Jack's urine and the blue bag.)*

JACK LOVINGTON. I don't get why all the Bomber matches gotta be fixed, Lenny. It don't seem right. Me and Charlie could win 'em for real.

LENNY RINGLE. Real don't sell soap, kid. Real don't pay the bills. You know what real gets you? Pain. You wanna give the people pain?

JACK LOVINGTON. I guess not.

LENNY RINGLE. Of course not. You wanna give 'em joy. A happy ending every time. And that's what we do. Buy your ticket at the gate, buy yourself a smile. Turn on the tube, turn off your troubles.

JACK LOVINGTON. I guess I never thought of it that way. It just felt a whole lot better that first night at the Armory.

LENNY RINGLE. Yeah, well things ain't always what they seem. But clear your mind of it, kid. You're a great skater, ain't nothing phony about that. *(Dr. Seymour Friedman pops his head in. Another black man with a Jewish name.)*

DR. FRIEDMAN. Hello, I'm Dr. Seymour Friedman. Lovington, right?

JACK LOVINGTON. That's me, Doc.

DR. FRIEDMAN. Take your pants off, son. *(Doctor exits. Jack begins taking his pants off.)*

JACK LOVINGTON. And I don't know why you went and traded her to the Four-Wheelers, Lenny.

LENNY RINGLE. Had to do it, kid. Too much star power on one bus. I was getting killed on the other half of the tour.

JACK LOVINGTON. I can't stop thinking about her.

LENNY RINGLE. We needed her up north again. No one works a crowd like she does. But Lindy's a crazy kid, she's a noodle. You'll thank me for it later.

JACK LOVINGTON. You don't know her like I do, Lenny.

LENNY RINGLE. *(Laughs.)* You're too pure, kid. She don't deserve you.

JACK LOVINGTON. I don't think she gots self-love enough, that's all. Lindy needs someone to love her good.

LENNY RINGLE. She's a slut, kid. Trust me.

JACK LOVINGTON. I wish you wouldn't say that.

LENNY RINGLE. Sorry, kid, but look around you. Why the hell you think we here?

JACK LOVINGTON. This don't make no difference. I saw her heart, Lenny. She don't show that to no one else.

42

LENNY RINGLE. Yeah, well if she ain't showing her heart she's showing a lot of other things. Ask your penis. *(The nurse reenters.)*

LENNY RINGLE. Hey nurse, could we speed this up? We got a game in half an hour.

NURSE. Yeah. *(To Jack.)* Do you think you could pee for me again? I had an accident.

JACK LOVINGTON. I don't think so.

NURSE. Okay. Ah. Don't tell the doctor, okay? Just take your shorts off. *(The nurse exits.)*

LENNY RINGLE. Look kid, it's a five cent story. You get drunk. She pops your cherry. You wake up, you think it's love, she's out the door throwing her carpet at the first guy with two nickels to rub together.

JACK LOVINGTON. That's ten cents.

LENNY RINGLE. Same thing.

JACK LOVINGTON. What we had was beautiful.

LENNY RINGLE. What you had was a one-nighter.

JACK LOVINGTON. She told me she loved me.

LENNY RINGLE. Everybody loves everybody. That's the derby, kid! She loves you. She loves him. He loves her. Pretty soon we all got swollen dicks.

JACK LOVINGTON. Yeah? Well, this is different. I know how she feels. I seen her heart, Lenny.

LENNY RINGLE. Yeah, well wait three weeks, you can see her again in New York. *(Jack pulls down his shorts. Lenny leaps back.)* Jesus Christ, Lovington!

JACK LOVINGTON. What? It's not that bad. *(The doctor enters, wearing rubber gloves. Sees Jack's penis.)*

DR. FRIEDMAN. My god!

JACK LOVINGTON. What? What's wrong?

LENNY RINGLE. What the hell's he got there, doc?

DR. FRIEDMAN. I'm not entirely sure.

LENNY RINGLE. Christ on a cross.

JACK LOVINGTON. Lenny, could you stop saying that!

LENNY RINGLE. *(To Doctor.)* A Catholic boy.

DR. FRIEDMAN. Aren't they all? Nurse! *(To Jack.)* You're lucky that didn't fall off, son. *(The nurse enters. She screams. Jack tries to cover himself.)*

JACK LOVINGTON. Hey.

DR. FRIEDMAN. Nurse! Control yourself.

NURSE. Sorry, Doctor.

DR. FRIEDMAN. I'm going to need the blue bag and some rubbing alcohol.

NURSE. Yes, doctor. *(The nurse runs out. the doctor walks over to Jack.)*

LENNY RINGLE. What's with the barnacles, Doc?

DR. FRIEDMAN. What? You mean all these? *(The doctor starts poking Jack's penis.)*

JACK LOVINGTON. Ow. Ow. Ow. Ow.

DR. FRIEDMAN. They're called SIN!

JACK LOVINGTON. Huh?!

DR. FRIEDMAN. No, no, no. I'm just kidding. No, they're called genital warts, friend.

LENNY RINGLE. Didn't I tell you, kid?

JACK LOVINGTON. Is that why it hurts to go to the bathroom? *(The nurse reenters, trembling, with a red bag.)*

DR. FRIEDMAN. Just a second. *(To Nurse.)* I said the blue bag.

NURSE. You don't want the blue bag.

DR. FRIEDMAN. Why not?

NURSE. *(Looks at Jack.)* I spilled something on the blue bag.

DR. FRIEDMAN. Fine. Fine. Give me that. Get the pills ready. *(The nurse exits. The doctor pulls out a number of threatening needles and syringes.)* The answer to your question is no. The burning sensation you have is from gonorrhea. Perhaps syphilis. Your unusually large and bountiful warts are completely independent from your scorched urinary tract.

JACK LOVINGTON. Is this gonna hurt, doc?

DR. FRIEDMAN. Not at all son. What's your name, friend?

LENNY RINGLE. Lenny Ringle.

DR. FRIEDMAN. You don't look like a Ringle.

LENNY RINGLE. You don't look like a Friedman. *(They look at each other for a brief moment.)*

LENNY RINGLE AND DR. FRIEDMAN. Rigghhhtttt.

DR. FRIEDMAN. Leonard, would you be so kind as to restrain your friend, here.

LENNY RINGLE. Whatever you say, Seymour. *(Charlie grabs Jack's arms. The nurse reenters with two pill bottles.)*

DR. FRIEDMAN. Thank you. Nurse, here. *(The doctor hands the nurse a wooden stick.)* Now, son I have some antibiotics here. I want you to take two of these daily for the next three weeks. Try and take them with a meal, otherwise they're likely to rip a hole through your stomach.

JACK LOVINGTON. I gotta get a letter to her, Lenny. A love letter.

LENNY RINGLE. She ain't a lover letter girl. Trust me. What's with the syringe, doc?

DR. FRIEDMAN. This isn't a syringe. It's a soldering iron.

JACK LOVINGTON. What?!

DR. FRIEDMAN. Nurse. *(Nurse puts the stick in front of Jack's mouth.)*

NURSE. Open your mouth.

DR. FRIEDMAN. Jack, I want you to bite down on that stick.

JACK LOVINGTON. Oh, God. *(He bites down on the stick.)*

LENNY RINGLE. Take it like a man, kid. *(Jack screams. Lights down. We hear a doop-wop gem, like "Speedo" by the Cadillacs.* Lights up on Bert Fineberg and "Larry Calloway.")*

BERT FINEBERG. Bert Fineberg LIVE trackside, in the middle of period six here at the Philadelphia Spectrum. Bombers twenty-two, Pioneers nineteen! Non-stop action in America's filthiest, most God-forsaken city. Jack Lovington, the Bomber from Brooklyn, skating a little more gingerly than normal, moving up on Pioneer jammer, Specs Macedo. *(Bert exits. Jack Lovington wearing his Bombers jersey and "Specs" Macedo wearing a Pioneers jersey. They are in the middle of a vicious jam, skaters' bodies flying to the left and right of them.)*

JACK LOVINGTON. Specs?!

SPECS MACEDO. *(Muttering to himself.)* Stay on your feet, Specs!

JACK LOVINGTON. I gotta talk to you, Specs …

SPECS MACEDO. *(Muttering.)* No Brodies, no Brodies!

JACK LOVINGTON. You're skating versus the Four-Wheelers in Boston next week right?

SPECS MACEDO. Yeah. So what?

JACK LOVINGTON. So could you give this to Miss Batello? *(Jack pulls out a love letter on red stationery.)*

SPECS MACEDO. What?!

JACK LOVINGTON. I wrote her this letter. I need to get it to her.

SPECS MACEDO. We're in the middle of jam. Keep your head in the game, rookie! *(He smashes Jack in the face with and elbow. Jack fades back but maintains his balance.)*

JACK LOVINGTON. Watch out for the elbow!

SPECS MACEDO. Huh? Oh. *(He ducks under Jerry Kiger's flying elbow.)* Fucking degenerate! Thanks. *(Jack does the same.)*

---

* See Special Note on Songs and Recordings on copyright page.

JERRY KIGER. Whattya you warning him for?!

JACK LOVINGTON. Sorry, Jerry!

JERRY KIGER. *(Fading back.)* Keep your head in the game, rookie.

SPECS MACEDO. Lindy Batello?!

JACK LOVINGTON. She the one, Specs! The only girl for me!

SPECS MACEDO. Didn't she give you gonorrhea, kid?

JACK LOVINGTON. I can't stop thinking about her.

SPECS MACEDO. It's probably 'cause your urine burns. Get another shot in your dick and forget about it.

JACK LOVINGTON. Could you just give her the letter, please, Specs? *(He rips the letter from Jack's hand, stuffs it down his uniform.)*

SPECS MACEDO. Fine.

JACK LOVINGTON. Thanks, Specs.

SPECS MACEDO. I gotta shove you over the rail now, Jack.

JACK LOVINGTON. Okay. *(Specs violently shoves Jack over the railing. Specs races ahead. Bert Fineberg enters with cut-out Larry Calloway.)*

BERT FINEBERG. And we're back in Boston, Beantown, the town that hasn't had joy since 1918, LIVE with "SPECS" MACEDO getting chased by Londoner Olice Strayhorn. Just two weeks away from the Roller Derby Championship at Madison Square Garden, folks. Good seats still available and every seat's a great one! Isn't that right, Larry Calloway? *(Olice Strayhorn, a member of the Four-Wheelers, skates up next to Specs Macedo.)*

SPECS MACEDO. Strayhorn!

OLICE STRAYHORN. Hullo, Specs.

BERT FINEBERG. Are you ever gonna say anything, Larry? *(Bert Fineberg exits with Larry Calloway.)*

SPECS MACEDO. I didn't know you were on the Four-Wheelers.

OLICE STRAYHORN. I was on the Bombers last week and the Stranglers the week before. I don't get attached, know what I mean?

SPECS MACEDO. Yeah. Hey, could you give this to Batello.

OLICE STRAYHORN. What's this then?

SPECS MACEDO. It's from Lovington.

OLICE STRAYHORN. Redhead on the Bombers?

SPECS MACEDO. That's the one.

OLICE STRAYHORN. Nice bloke. What's he want with Batello?

SPECS MACEDO. A one way ticket to H-E-double hockey sticks.

OLICE STRAYHORN. Indeed. Alright, why don't you throw me into the pit?

SPECS MACEDO. Right now?

OLICE STRAYHORN. Why not? The match is bollocks.

SPECS MACEDO. Okay, man. *(Specs punches Strayhorn in the face and skates offstage. Strayhorn waves his arms wildly and the two lady Four-Wheelers come onstage.)*

CINDY GUMS. Yeah this time of month, I bleed like a mother-fucker.

LINDY BATELLO. Yeah, well at least you're bleeding. I'm two fucking weeks late. I'm never late. *(Strayhorn lands on his back, at the feet of Cindy Gums and Lindy Batello.)*

OLICE STRAYHORN. *(Handing her the letter.)* It's for you. *(Olice collapses.)*

LINDY BATELLO. What the fuck? *(A track medical attendant enters stage, checks Olice. Lindy hands Cindy Gums the letter.)* Probably more hate mail. Read it to me. *(Cindy Gums rips open the red love letter.)*

TRACK MEDICAL ATTENDANT. CONCUSSION! *(The attendant drags Olice's body offstage.)*

CINDY GUMS. *(Reading.)* Dear Lindy. My pencil is down to a nub, my fingertips are raw from failure, underneath my shirt pocket, the heart of a scarecrow. I cannot find the just-right words to blanket your slight shivers, the all-knowing gestures to warm you. Two weeks ago, our night together transformed me and I haven't touched the ground ever since. I am like a rocket, blasting off to the moon, blazing, fevered and ultimately earthbound, waiting for your timely rescue. This letter speeds to you. Jack Lovington. *(She puts down the letter.)* I think he likes you.

LINDY BATELLO. Yeah, it's kinda nice, huh?

CINDY GUMS. You like him? *(Lenny walks by. Lindy sees him.)*

LINDY BATELLO. I don't like nobody. Lenny, you got a pen?

LENNY RINGLE. You gonna stab someone in the eye with it?

LINDY BATELLO. No, I'm taking up figure drawing. Hand it over. *(He gives her a pen.)*

LENNY RINGLE. Nice five-stride out there, Gums.

CINDY GUMS. Thanks, Lenny.

LINDY BATELLO. Yeah, thanks Lenny. *(To Cindy Gums.)* Turn around. *(Lindy starts writing on the envelope of Jack's love letter against Cindy's back.)* Hey, ratface. Your slut girlfriend "Big Tickets" Moreland?

LENNY RINGLE. Yeah, what about her?

LINDY BATELLO. She skating against the Bombers next week?

LENNY RINGLE. No, the Pioneers are with you guys again. The Bombers are in New Haven against the Stranglers.

LINDY BATELLO. Trade her to the Stranglers.

LENNY RINGLE. Why should I?

LINDY BATELLO. 'Cause Lovington's becoming a real pain in my ass. You didn't pay me enough when you pimped me out.

LENNY RINGLE. Funny, I remember you volunteering for the job. *(We hear the referee's whistle.)*

LINDY BATELLO. Trade her!

LENNY RINGLE. The pen! *(She gives him the pen. she gives Cindy Gums the folded envelope, and stuffs Jack's love letter inside her uniform.)*

LINDY BATELLO. Get this to "Big Tickets." Tell her to get it to Howdy-Doody.

LENNY RINGLE. Get in there girls! I don't pay you to look nice. *(Lenny Ringle exits. Cindy Gums skates onto the track. Bert Fineberg enters.)*

BERT FINEBERG. The Ladies taking the track in what we can only hope is a more exciting period than the men's was. Telling it like it is, roller fans. Telling it like is. *(Bert Fineberg exits. The Carol "Big Tickets" cut-out comes onstage.)*

CINDY GUMS. Carol. Carol. Stupid cardboard, look at me. You got to get this to Jack Lovington on the Bombers. *(She tries to hand the letter to the cut-out, which obviously cannot "take it." Cindy Gums, ever clever, pulls out her chewing gum, attaches it to the letter and smacks it onto the cut-out. She gives the audience a sheepish smile and skates off.)*

BERT FINEBERG. Carol Moreland newly traded to the Stranglers. *(A Strangler jersey is slapped onto Carol "Big Tickets.")* Skating her heart out here at the New Haven Coliseum! Scoreboard here in New Haven says, oh yes, and like everything else in this Ivy League town the scoreboard is broken. *(Making it up.)* Bombers twenty-one, Stranglers eighteen with Nutterman inching up to Moreland. *(Beth Nutterman "skates" onstage.)*

BETH NUTTERMAN. Hear there's a new bar opened up in town for girls like us, Carol. How 'bout I pick you up at the motel? Great! Huh? Oh, alright. *(She takes the letter from Carol. Looks at the chewing gum on the back, shrugs and puts it in her mouth. We hear the referee's whistle. The girls slow down and wait for the men to join them on the track.)*

BERT FINEBERG. Change-over into the four period and time now for a word from tonight's sponsor. *(Jack Lovington "skates" next to Beth Nutterman. Charlie Heartbreak, behind Jack.)*

BETH NUTTERMAN. It's for you, kid.

JACK LOVINGTON. Oh boy. Gee, thanks, Nutterman. *(Beth*

Nutterman skates off.)

BERT FINEBERG. Mr. and Mrs. Smith, when was the last time you tried Ramco's Farm Fresh Goat Margarine? The butter substitute that's all the rage from Main St. to Madison Avenue … *(Bert Fineberg exits. Jack looks around, opening the letter away from the other skaters.)*

JACK LOVINGTON. *(Reading the letter.)* Dear Creep. Fruity words don't mean shit, jack. It's just one sick-o night pretending I'm someone else. Get over it. Fuck yourself with a stick. Lindy.

CHARLIE HEARTBREAK. I think she likes you.

JACK LOVINGTON. *(Reading.)* P.S. I think I'm pregnant. We gotta talk.

CHARLIE HEARTBREAK. Charlie's gonna pretend he didn't hear that. *(Jack looks horrified and heartsick. We hear the referee's whistle blow. Lights down. Lights up on Father Kosciusko in his office, reading a Spanish primer called* Juan y Maria.*)*

FATHER KOSCIUSKO. Juan and Maria went to the zoo to see a monkey. *(He shuts the book, closes his eyes.) Juan y María fueron al zoológico a ver un mono. (He opens the book.)* Hmmm. Juan and Maria talked to a man about a car. They're not even old enough to drive. *(He shuts the book.) Juan y María hablaron con un hombre acerca de un carro. (The phone rings.)* Who's calling at this hour? *(He answers the phone.) Hola,* Saint Barbara's? Baltimore? Who? Yes, I'll accept the charges. Or wait, wait. *Sí, acepto los cargos.* Nothing. Just go ahead, operator. Jack? *(Lights up on Jack Lovington in a phone booth at a bus station.)*

JACK LOVINGTON. Forgive me, Father, for I have sinned. It's been over three months since my last confession.

FATHER KOSCIUSKO. *Confiesa, hijo mío.*

JACK LOVINGTON. Father Domingo?

FATHER KOSCIUSKO. No, Jack it's me. I'm practicing my Spanish. And I'm pretty good, aren't I, Juan and Maria?

JACK LOVINGTON. Who's Juan and Maria?

FATHER KOSCIUSKO. A little gift from Archbishop McCullough, who apparently doesn't think I'm accessible enough to my congregation. Doesn't think I'm capable of change, of reaching out.

JACK LOVINGTON. So he sent you two children named Juan and Maria?

FATHER KOSCIUSKO. Never mind, Jack. Why are you calling so late? Are you okay?

JACK LOVINGTON. Yeah, I'm sorry about that. Someone stole the car battery out of the bus while we was going to the bathroom.

Baltimore's a tough town. I'll be home tomorrow ...

FATHER KOSCIUSKO. The Roller Derby Championship?

JACK LOVINGTON. Yeah. And sorry for calling collect. I ain't got paid in two weeks, Father. I just couldn't wait no longer. I had to talk to someone before I talked to someone.

FATHER KOSCIUSKO. Say again.

JACK LOVINGTON. I'm in trouble, Father.

FATHER KOSCIUSKO. What is it, my son?

JACK LOVINGTON. I think I might have gotten someone pregnant.

FATHER KOSCIUSKO. *(Sighs.)* Yes. Seems there's a lot of that going around.

JACK LOVINGTON. Did you hear what I said, Father?

FATHER KOSCIUSKO. Is this the girl you're "unbearably in love with"?

JACK LOVINGTON. Well, I don't know about that. I mean, yeah, I guess. I'm a little confused right now, Father.

FATHER KOSCIUSKO. Is it Cindy Gums?

JACK LOVINGTON. Huh?

FATHER KOSCIUSKO. Carol Moreland?

JACK LOVINGTON. No, Father. How come you know them people? How come you know about the Championship?

FATHER KOSCIUSKO. All part of the new reaching out. Putting yourself in the shoes of your flock, as the Archbishop calls it. I thought maybe I'd been too hard on you, Jack. So I watched the roller derby, a couple weeks ago.

JACK LOVINGTON. You did?

FATHER KOSCIUSKO. Oh yes. Grown adults running around in a circle, smashing each other in the face! The spongy short-pants, the tight blouses accentuating overdeveloped breasts! Yes, Jack, I watch the roller derby and I lacerate myself with a curtain rod for five minutes each time I do. *(Beth Nutterman enters.)*

BETH NUTTERMAN. Hey Jack, hurry up.

JACK LOVINGTON. Hold on, Father.

BETH NUTTERMAN. Charlie found the guy who stole the car battery. He kicked his ass the whole time while he made the guy put it back in. *(She exits. Jack nods "okay.")*

JACK LOVINGTON. Father ...

FATHER KOSCIUSKO. Don't get me wrong. There are some things I'm trying to enjoy about it. Like that Beth Nutterman. I like that girl. She's got spirit. Is she the girl, Jack?

JACK LOVINGTON. No, Father. *(We hear the bus engine start, a horn sounds.)* Ah jeez. There's the bus. I didn't even get to start my confession or nothing.

FATHER KOSCIUSKO. Jack, I'll tell you the same thing I told Aurora, Jack. You need to take responsibility for your actions.

JACK LOVINGTON. How come you say that to Aurora?

FATHER KOSCIUSKO. Let's just say she's in a similar situation as yourself, Jack.

JACK LOVINGTON. Oh she is, is she? Yeah, well she got Al Deepadova to look after her now.

FATHER KOSCIUSKO. Yes, well, no one seems to know where Alfonse is. Seems he's nowhere to be found.

JACK LOVINGTON. What? *(We hear the sound of the bus horn again.)* Hold on a second. *(Into the phone.)* Is she okay?

FATHER KOSCIUSKO. Good luck tomorrow, Jack. We'll talk more when you get home. *(Lights out on Father Kosciusko. One more bus horn.)*

JACK LOVINGTON. I'm coming, Lenny. *(Jack runs offstage with his suitcase. Lights up on a chartered bus. The female bus driver is at the helm trying to keep her eyes open. The team is asleep. Lenny Ringle is up front, staring straight ahead. Jack is muttering to himself, dreaming. It sounds like a nightmare. After a moment, he wakes up. Waking up:)* Rib truck!

LENNY RINGLE. Shhhh.

JACK LOVINGTON. Huh?

LENNY RINGLE. You were dreaming. Morning, kid.

JACK LOVINGTON. Where's the sun?

LENNY RINGLE. Hiding behind the Chrysler building.

JACK LOVINGTON. Where's Lindy?

LENNY RINGLE. In the back. You were asleep when we got into Philly.

JACK LOVINGTON. Oh.

LENNY RINGLE. Still got a thing for her, huh, kid?

JACK LOVINGTON. I gots to talk to her.

LENNY RINGLE. Yeah, well, she was in no mood to talk when we picked her up. Better let her sleep. *(The bus driver closes her eyes.)*

JACK LOVINGTON. Where are we?

LENNY RINGLE. Home. Take a look at it, kid. *(Jack gets up, walks to Lenny. he looks out, his eyes get big.)*

JACK LOVINGTON. Wow!

LENNY RINGLE. Beautiful, ain't it?

JACK LOVINGTON. Madison Square Garden.

LENNY RINGLE. And one day you're gonna skate there, kid. I just know it.

JACK LOVINGTON. Yeah. Tonight's gonna be great. Hey how come they got the circus on the marquee there, Lenny?

LENNY RINGLE. Over one hundred live camels. Well, I'll be damned.

JACK LOVINGTON. Hey, how come we ain't stopping, Lenny? *(The bus driver opens her eyes suddenly.)*

FEMALE BUS DRIVER. Go, Bears!

LENNY RINGLE. You okay, driver?

FEMALE BUS DRIVER. Oh, sure.

JACK LOVINGTON. She passed the Garden, Lenny.

LENNY RINGLE. Huh? Oh, hey, almost forgot. Here. *(He hands Jack an envelope.)*

JACK LOVINGTON. What's this?

LENNY RINGLE. It's for the last two weeks. And for tonight. The last of the TV money. Lenny Ringle pays his debts.

JACK LOVINGTON. We ain't skating for no championship, are we?

LENNY RINGLE. Hell yes, we're skating. I sold nine hundred tickets for the damn thing. Damn right we're skating. Just not at the Garden. We're back in Coney Island. At the Armory. *(The driver starts slapping herself to stay awake.)*

LENNY RINGLE. Driver?

FEMALE BUS DRIVER. I'm okay. I like doing this.

JACK LOVINGTON. What happened, Lenny?

LENNY RINGLE. Our ratings were bupkis, kid. They're replacing us with some quiz show. The suits told me the sport was too dark.

JACK LOVINGTON. What's that mean, Lenny?

LENNY RINGLE. Nothing kid. *(Pause.)* They hated us in Champaigne, Illinois.

FEMALE BUS DRIVER. I'm from Champaigne.

JACK LOVINGTON. That's okay, Lenny. I'd skate even if I wasn't on no TV.

LENNY RINGLE. Well, you're gonna have to skate for crackers then, there ain't no more cheese.

JACK LOVINGTON. Yeah. Now we can skate for real, Lenny. We don't have to fix it up or nothing. Just like that first night I skated. *(Lenny starts laughing. Lindy wakes up in the back, listens.)* What's so funny?

LENNY RINGLE. *(Laughing.)* You're too pure, kid. The cream at the top of the milk bottle.

JACK LOVINGTON. *(Laughing.)* What? I don't even like milk.

LENNY RINGLE. *(Laughing.)* Ah, kid, I hate to break it to you but that night at the Armory was rigged too. I had them guys taking Brodies left and right.

JACK LOVINGTON. Say it ain't so, Lenny.

LENNY RINGLE. The name ain't Lenny, kid. That's a fact. It's Reginal. Reginal Robinson. And the fact of it is, no TV, no derby. 'Cause the derby's a show and not a sport and 'cause you can put a Robinson at second base for the Dodgers but you need a Ringle behind the owner's desk at the derby. So that money ain't from the TV 'cause we ain't been on TV for two weeks. That's a fact. That money came from a warehouse in Newark where a good friend of mine gives great loans at forty percent on the dollar. So keep your chin up, kid, you're a great skater, except when you're thinking about that girl you got at home, so Lindy's not really in love with you, 'cause I paid her to sleep with you. Nothing is as it seems, kid. That twinkling light up there could be a morning star or it could be that Sputnik satellite. So skate like I tell you to, today. And then go back to your church and your yellow cab, and I'll call you in six months when I got it up and running again. 'Cause if there's one fact in the world, one thing you can count on, it's that the derby ain't dead long as there's people like you and me who believe in it.

JACK LOVINGTON. What's your name, again? *(The bus driver starts slapping her face again.)*

LENNY RINGLE. Reginal. Reginal Robinson. Nice to meet you, Jack. *(Lights down. We hear fifties TV show orchestral music.)*

FIFTIES TV ANNOUNCER VOICE. It's time … It's time … It's time for … It's time for *Your Money … or Your Wife!* America's newest, most hilarious new newlewyed quiz show. With your host, Marvin Mercury. And now for the program that asks the question you ask yourself every time you leave the house … *Your Money … or Your Wife! (Orchestral music cross fades into the sound of a roller coaster. Lights up on Lindy Batello, drinking from a flask, sitting in the front car of Coney Island's famous "Cyclone" rollercoaster. She's wearing her Four-Wheeler jersey, trying to make conversation with the scared kid sitting next to her. Other riders sit in the cars behind her.)*

LINDY BATELLO. I was tired, see. Just couldn't pick up my face anymore. So Lenny checked me in. But then he busted me out so don't have to go back if I don't want to. You understand what I'm fucking saying? *(The ride hits a big dip. A few in the car stick their hands up and scream.)* Whhheeeeeeeeeeeeeeeeeeewwwwwwwwwwwwwwwwwwwww! I love that fucking one. That's a good one, huh? *(She takes a swig from her flask.)* Where was I? You wanna a swig, Junior? *(The kid shakes his head.)* Yeah, you're too young. I'm never too young. Here come the whoopsies. Get ready, Junior. *(The ride hits a few hills.)* Whoopsie. Whoopsie. Whoopsie. Whhhhhhheeeeeeeeeewwwwwww. Now we having some fun, eh Junior? More fun than a fucking hospital, I'll tell you that. *(The ride stops.)*

SCARED KID'S MOM. Ginny. Ginny.

LINDY BATELLO. Ginny? I thought your name was Junior?

SCARED KID'S MOM. Get away from that lady.

RIDE OPERATOR. Everybody out. Everyone on. *(Riders exit off-stage, except for Lindy. New riders on. No one sits next to Lindy, who pulls out a quarter.)*

LINDY BATELLO. Good kid there, mom. You got a winner.

RIDE OPERATOR. Twenty-five cents.

LINDY BATELLO. Another go around, chiefie.

JACK LOVINGTON. *(Offstage.)* LINDY!

RIDE OPERATOR. Twenty-five cents, babydoll. *(She forks over the twenty-five cents. Jack enters, wearing his Bombers jersey.)*

JACK LOVINGTON. Lindy!

LINDY BATELLO. Start the fucking ride, chiefie!

JACK LOVINGTON. Lindy, what are you doing?! I been looking for you everywheres!

LINDY BATELLO. I'm riding the roller coaster, Howdy-Doody.

RIDE OPERATOR. The Cyclone cost a quarter, buddy.

JACK LOVINGTON. We got the championship in an hour, Lindy!

LINDY BATELLO. Jack it up, chiefie!

RIDE OPERATOR. Twenty-five cents or twenty-five paces.

ANGRY ROLLER COASTER RIDER. Make a decision, Bomber boy.

JACK LOVINGTON. I'm sorry. I only got fives. *(Jack gives the ride operator a five dollar bill, then gets into the seat next to Lindy.)*

RIDE OPERATOR. We take fives. Ride all you want, buddy.

LINDY BATELLO. Get this. This is the best part.

RIDE OPERATOR. *(Shouting.)* Jack it up!

LINDY BATELLO. *(Shouting.)* Jack it up! That right, chiefie! *(The ride starts up on a climb.)*

JACK LOVINGTON. How come you been avoiding me?

LINDY BATELLO. I don't know what you're talking about. *(She*

takes a swig from her flask.)
JACK LOVINGTON. You said on the envelope we gotta talk. Then I tries to talk to you and you keep running away or calling me a faggot and we only got an hour before we gotta lace 'em up. *(The ride reaches the crest.)*
LINDY BATELLO. Hands up!
JACK LOVINGTON. Huh?
LINDY BATELLO. *(Pointing down.)* Hands up, faggot. *(Jack looks down. the ride plummets down. Everyone screams, especially, Jack.)* Whhheeeeeeeeeeeewwwwwwwwwwwwww. *(The ride straightens out, but still at a crazy velocity.)*
JACK LOVINGTON. I hate these rides.
LINDY BATELLO. These got two big dips and a couple of whoopsies, it's better than a fucking cornfield.
JACK LOVINGTON. We gotta talk.
LINDY BATELLO. What we gotta talk about? *(The ride climbs up again.)*
JACK LOVINGTON. How about what you said on this envelope, huh? *(He pulls out the envelope.)*
LINDY BATELLO. How about what you said inside the envelope? *(She pulls out the letter.)*

JACK LOVINGTON.
Just one sick-o night pretending I'm someone else. Get over it. Fuck yourself with a stick. Lindy. P.S. I think I'm pregnant. We gotta talk. What do you mean?

LINDY BATELLO.
I am like a fucking rocket. Blazing and fevered and earthsomething. Waiting for you to rescue me. This letter whatever and a stick. Jack Lovington. What the fuck is that all about?

(The ride hits a big dip. Jack screams.)
LINDY BATELLO. Whhhheeeeeeeeeeeewwwwwwwwwwwwwww.
JACK LOVINGTON. You're pregnant?
LINDY BATELLO. You in love with me or something?
JACK LOVINGTON. Yeah, I guess.
LINDY BATELLO. Go fuck yourself, Howdy-Doody!
ANGRY ROLLER COASTER RIDER. Watch your language up there. *(She spits back at him, hitting him in the eye.)*
JACK LOVINGTON. You shouldn't spit on people. I'm sorry, mister.
ANGRY ROLLER COASTER RIDER. You got some nerve lady.
LINDY BATELLO. *(Pushing him.)* What do you mean, I guess?

This letter don't say I guess. *(The ride hits a few hills.)*

JACK LOVINGTON. Stop hitting me. I meant that letter.

LINDY BATELLO. I guess? Fuck you. You're like everyone else. Everyone wants a hunk of me.

JACK LOVINGTON. Are you gonna have baby?

LINDY BATELLO. No. I'm not gonna have a baby. *(The ride slows down. Jack looks relieved.)*

JACK LOVINGTON. Phew. *(Lindy hits him in the jaw.)* What did you do that for?!

LINDY BATELLO. 'Cause I coulda had a baby, asshole.

JACK LOVINGTON. What?

LINDY BATELLO. Fucking glad I didn't.

LENNY RINGLE. *(Offstage.)* Lindy! Jack! *(The ride stops. The operator appears.)*

RIDE OPERATOR. Everybody out. Everyone on. *(The riders get out including Jack. New ones come on, one of them is Lenny.)*

JACK LOVINGTON. What do you mean, you coulda had a baby?!

LINDY BATELLO. I got rid of it. Back in Philadelphia.

LENNY RINGLE. What the hell are you doing on this thing, Lindy?! *(Lindy gives the operator a quarter.)*

LINDY BATELLO. Another go around, chiefie.

LENNY RINGLE. No way. We gotta go!

JACK LOVINGTON. *(To Lindy.)* What?

LENNY RINGLE. Jack, help me get her out.

RIDE OPERATOR. Getting in costs a quarter buddy.

JACK LOVINGTON. *(To Lindy.)* How could you do that?!

LINDY BATELLO. Jack it up, chiefie!

LENNY RINGLE. Lindy!

LINDY BATELLO. I ain't leaving this car.

LENNY RINGLE. Lindy, we got a game about to go on.

JACK LOVINGTON. That's the worst thing I ever heard in my life, Lindy!

LINDY BATELLO. I ain't going back to that hospital, Lenny.

JACK LOVINGTON. That wasn't your right to do that!

RIDE OPERATOR. Now or never, pal.

LENNY RINGLE. All's I got is a five. *(Lenny Ringle gives the operator a five dollar bill. Gets into the seat next to Lindy.)*

RIDE OPERATOR. We take fives. Jack it up. *(Jack gets into one of the back cars. The ride climbs up.)*

LENNY RINGLE. Who said anything about you going back to

the hospital?

LINDY BATELLO. Liar! Fucking fat-ass liar!

JACK LOVINGTON. Lindy, we ain't through talking!

LENNY RINGLE. Shut up, kid!

JACK LOVINGTON. No, you shut up, Lenny!

LENNY RINGLE. What did you say, kid?!

JACK LOVINGTON. I said shut up! She's right! You're a liar! *(The ride reaches its crest.)*

LINDY BATELLO. You tell 'em, Howdy-Doody!

JACK LOVINGTON. And so are you, Lindy! And stop calling me that! *(The ride plummets. Everyone sticks their hands up and screams.)*

LINDY BATELLO. Whhheeeeeeeeeeeeeeeewwwwwwwwwwwww. *(She takes another swig from her flask. The ride straightens out.)*

LENNY RINGLE. Watch what you say back there, Lovington!

LINDY BATELLO. Yeah, you're getting a fucking mouth on you!

LENNY RINGLE. You don't know everything I done for you. What I got to do to keep the derby going, kid! I care about you!

JACK LOVINGTON. I know he paid you to be with me, Lindy! *(Lindy looks at Lenny.)*

LENNY RINGLE. Oh goddamn. *(She hits him in the jaw.)*

LINDY BATELLO. You fink!

JACK LOVINGTON. I been nice to both of youse! *(The ride climbs up again.)*

LINDY BATELLO. How come you got to louse everything up, Lenny?

JACK LOVINGTON. His name's Reginal! You remember that name, huh, Lindy?!

LINDY BATELLO. I don't feel so good.

JACK LOVINGTON. It's you two used to go out with each other, right?! I ain't so smart but I ain't dumb! I ain't dumb no more, Lindy! So don't go getting all angry at me when I go to say "I guess" I love you. You're lucky I got any feelings for you at all after what you done! You're a whore! *(The riders gasp, shocked. the ride reaches its crest.)*

LINDY BATELLO. I'm gonna be sick.

LENNY RINGLE. You're going down a blind alley, kid!

JACK LOVINGTON. No! She's the one going down alleys, Lenny! Tell him Lindy! *(The ride plummets.)*

LENNY RINGLE. I already know about that, kid.

JACK LOVINGTON. What?! *(Lindy turns around and throws up. The riders behind her duck, and the vomit hits Jack in the face.)* Ah jeez. *(The ride straightens out, Jack wipes off the vomit.)* How come he knows before I do, Lindy?!

LENNY RINGLE. Who the hell you think paid for it? Huh, kid? You gotta believe me when I tell you I care about you, kid. You don't love Lindy. Come on, look at her. You gotta think about yourself in this, Jack. You gotta be more selfish. You gotta future in this game. *(The ride hits the hills again.)* You don't want some crap-making machine tying you down! And you certainly don't want it with some out-of-her-mind girl gonna be going in and out of nut houses her whole life. What kind of mother was she gonna be?

LINDY BATELLO. You fucking rat.

LENNY RINGLE. I'm been taking care of her for years. I know what she needs. And she don't need you filling her head with love letters you ain't never gonna be able to back up. *(The ride stops. the ride operator appears.)*

RIDE OPERATOR. Everybody out. Everyone on. *(Old riders out, including Lenny. One or two new riders in.)*

LENNY RINGLE. I care about you, kid. And I care about you too, Lindy. And you both know I'm right. Now come on.

LINDY BATELLO. I ain't going back to that hospital, Lenny. *(She hands the operator another quarter.)*

LENNY RINGLE. I'm talking about the Armory over there. We got fans in there waiting for a championship. Waiting for my two biggest stars!

RIDE OPERATOR. In or out?

LENNY RINGLE. They're out. Jack? What are you doing? *(Jack gets out of the back of the car.)*

RIDE OPERATOR. Jack it up! *(Jack gets into the car behind Lindy. The ride climbs up.)*

LENNY RINGLE. Jack!

LINDY BATELLO. What are you doing?!

JACK LOVINGTON. We ain't through talking.

LENNY RINGLE. *(Offstage.)* You two got half an hour! I need you two! *(The ride reaches its crest. Dips over and plummets down. They ride quietly for a while.)*

LINDY BATELLO. I'm sorry about what I did. I didn't want to do it, you know? I thought about what you said in the letter. I thought about maybe me and you could have something good.

JACK LOVINGTON. C'mon.

LINDY BATELLO. I fucking mean it. You gotta believe me. But I couldn't do it. The doctor said it was dangerous. I had some things wrong with me. You might wanna get yourself checked out. *(The*

ride climbs up again.)
JACK LOVINGTON. Oh.
LINDY BATELLO. Lenny's right, I ain't pure like you.
JACK LOVINGTON. Don't listen to what he says.
LINDY BATELLO. No, he's right.
JACK LOVINGTON. You're plenty good. *(The ride hits its crest.)*
LINDY BATELLO. Stop saying that shit. Stop saying nice things.
JACK LOVINGTON. I mean it.
LINDY BATELLO. I know you hate me. *(The ride plummets.)*
JACK LOVINGTON. I don't hate you, Lindy. *(They ride quietly for a while. Through the hills.)*
LINDY BATELLO. I'm sorry you found out I got paid. It didn't mean I wouldn't done it. I liked you. You were kind. And I'm sorry about what I wrote back to you. I really loved what you wrote in that letter. I didn't want no one to know how I felt. *(The ride slows down.)*
JACK LOVINGTON. I meant what I said in that letter. That night was beautiful. You put me back together again.
LINDY BATELLO. Yeah? Humpty Dumpty.
JACK LOVINGTON. Howdy-Doody. *(The ride stops. The ride operator appears.)*
RIDE OPERATOR. Everyone out. Everyone on.
JACK LOVINGTON. Hey. Here's ten bucks. Don't let no one else on. *(Jack moves up into the car seat next to Lindy.)*
RIDE OPERATOR. *(To the riders.)* What are ya, deaf? Everyone out. C'mon. *(The riders are shooed off. The ride operator removes all the chairs except Lindy and Jack.)*
RIDE OPERATOR. Jack it up! *(The ride begins to climb.)*
JACK LOVINGTON. Look. Alright, maybe things have been done wrong so far. Maybe everything in the world's been up against us saying we shouldn't be together.
LINDY BATELLO. What are you gonna fucking propose to me?
JACK LOVINGTON. Listen. It's okay what's happened. 'Cause I know it don't matter. 'Cause I really think I love you. *(The ride reaches its crest.)*
LINDY BATELLO. Shut up.
JACK LOVINGTON. Lindy, I'm serious.
LINDY BATELLO. Just shut the fuck up for a second. *(The ride plummets.)*
JACK LOVINGTON. Lindy …
LINDY BATELLO. I got something to say here … *(The ride straightens out.)* I want you to take this. *(She hands him the red love letter.)*

JACK LOVINGTON. That's yours.

LINDY BATELLO. Shut up for a second. Now look. No one ever wrote me such a nice thing in my life. No one. Not even Lenny back when he was Reginal. What you said in there was beautiful.

JACK LOVINGTON. I meant it.

LINDY BATELLO. Yeah. I know you did. *(Pause.)* But it ain't as good as this one. *(She pulls out the taped back together powder blue love letter he wrote to Aurora. The ride begins to climb.)* Yeah. I saved this one too. I carried it with me everywhere I went after that night. I looked at it every time I went to bed. I looked at it in the waiting room of the doctor's office. And I thought I could be with this guy forever. This is a real good person. He's a fucking prize, you know? You see, that letter, ain't like this letter. And this letter wasn't for me. *(The ride begins its crest.)* I don't know what's in that head of yours. But if I ever felt this way about somebody, I don't know what the hell I'd be doing with someone like me. *(The ride plummets, then straightens out.)* This is yours too. *(She gives him the powder blue love letter.)* Here come the whoopsies. *(The ride hits the hills again.)*

JACK LOVINGTON. She's pregnant you know? She had sex with someone else whiles I was gone.

LINDY BATELLO. So did you. *(The ride begins to slow down.)*

JACK LOVINGTON. You told me you loved me.

LINDY BATELLO. I did Jack. For one night, I really did.

JACK LOVINGTON. You don't love me now. *(The ride stops.)*

LINDY BATELLO. No. *(She kisses him. The ride operator enters.)*

RIDE OPERATOR. Everyone out. *(Lindy gets out.)*

LINDY BATELLO. I gotta go skate. It's what I do.

JACK LOVINGTON. Yeah. *(She exits.)*

RIDE OPERATOR. What's it gonna be, pal? *(Jack hands him another five.)* Jack it up. *(The operator removes the chair Lindy was sitting in. The ride begins to climb. Jack is alone. He stares out for a while as the ride continues its motions. At some point he looks down at the powder blue love letter. We begin to hear some church music. Buckets begin being placed onstage. Jack begins to mutter.)*

JACK LOVINGTON. And where there is darkness — light, where there is sadness, joy. O divine master, grant that I may not so much seek to be consoled as to console, to be understood as to understand ... *(Light change as the sound of the roller coaster fades out. Father Kosciusko enters quietly from behind wearing a New York Bombers jersey over his priest's outfit.)* ... to be loved as to love, for it is in giving that we receive, in pardoning that we are pardoned, and it is in dying that we are born into eternal love amen, the Father and the Son, and the Holy Ghost amen.

FATHER KOSCIUSKO. Amen. *(Jack Lovington looks back at him.)*

JACK LOVINGTON. Father. I let myself in.

FATHER KOSCIUSKO. It's nine-thirty, Jack. Shouldn't you be skating?

JACK LOVINGTON. Yeah.

FATHER KOSCIUSKO. But, it's the championship. Isn't the team depending on you?

JACK LOVINGTON. They'll be fine.

FATHER KOSCIUSKO. Fine time to just up and quit.

JACK LOVINGTON. Father, if you knew where I've been, you wouldn't say that. What are you wearing?

FATHER KOSCIUSKO. Oh. Well. *(He takes it off.)* I was walking by a novelty store and just happened to see this. Beth Nutterman's number. It's nothing really. *(The choir finishes.)*

JACK LOVINGTON. Choir sounds real good.

FATHER KOSCIUSKO. Yes. Father Domingo's got a real gift, you could say. What's that in your hand, Jack?

JACK LOVINGTON. Yeah. Don't look like much do it? Seen a lot, this piece of paper. *(We begin to hear the sound of light rain falling.)*

FATHER KOSCIUSKO. Certainly does look that way. *(Father Domingo walks by carrying a primer called* John and Marie.*)* How are you today, Father? *Muy bien, padre.*

JACK LOVINGTON. The choir sounds real good, Father Domingo.

FATHER DOMINGO. Yes. *(And with nothing else to say, he opens his primer and walks offstage. We begin to hear the occasional raindrop in a bucket.)* Juan y María disfrutan la habitación del motel. John and Marie enjoy the motel room.

JACK LOVINGTON. A lot more buckets around now.

FATHER KOSCIUSKO. Not for long, Jack. Father Domingo's services have become so popular, I think we're going to be able to purchase that new roof soon.

JACK LOVINGTON. That's great.

FATHER KOSCIUSKO. And that problem we talked about over the phone? With the other girl?

JACK LOVINGTON. Oh. Not what I thought it was.

FATHER KOSCIUSKO. I see. So no more roller derby, Jack?

JACK LOVINGTON. I don't know. Thought maybe I'd teach the orphans how to roller skate. Maybe start a little league in the neighborhood?

FATHER KOSCIUSKO. Sounds like an idea.

JACK LOVINGTON. I figure we could use the wood from the roof. I could build a track out in the common yard.

FATHER KOSCIUSKO. Sounds like a very thrifty idea. *(More raindrops.)*

JACK LOVINGTON. Would you hear my confession, Father?

FATHER KOSCIUSKO. What is it with you young people these days. Friday confession. Someone else came in here today asking for the same thing. A girl with a lot on her mind. Very busy. A real modern girl. I told her to come back tomorrow. Tomorrow's Saturday, I said. Better day for that kind of thing.

JACK LOVINGTON. Aurora?

FATHER KOSCIUSKO. She didn't tell me her name. Nice girl though. Works at a flower shop I believe. *(Father Kosciusko puts his hand on Jack's shoulder.)* Go home, Jack. Get some sleep. *(Slowly we begin to hear the sound of raindrops hitting buckets.)*

JACK LOVINGTON. Gotta do something about this roof, Father. *(Jack rises exits offstage.)*

FATHER KOSCIUSKO. All in good time, son. *(A pigeon lands on Father Kosciusko. He smiles at it. Moves it to his hand and takes the bird offstage. The raindrops continue, like so many canes tapping on a roof. The sound is beautiful, teeming with hope. A single door with an apartment number is slid onstage amongst the buckets. After a moment, Jack Lovington walks back onstage. The raindrops fade to a whisper. Jack walks up the door, knocks. He waits a moment.)*

VOICE OF AURORA. Who's there?

JACK LOVINGTON. It's me.

VOICE OF AURORA. What do you want?

JACK LOVINGTON. I want you back.

VOICE OF AURORA. Yeah? I heard you was in love with another girl.

JACK LOVINGTON. I thought I was in love.

VOICE OF AURORA. You ain't in love with her?

JACK LOVINGTON. No.

VOICE OF AURORA. *(Pause.)* I had sex with Al Deepadova.

JACK LOVINGTON. I know.

VOICE OF AURORA. I'm three months pregnant with his baby.

JACK LOVINGTON. I know.

VOICE OF AURORA. He skipped town and I don't know where he is.

JACK LOVINGTON. Do you love him?

VOICE OF AURORA. *(Pause.)* No.

JACK LOVINGTON. I want you back, Aurora. The baby's gonna need a father.

VOICE OF AURORA. Are you still roller-skating?

JACK LOVINGTON. I'm taking a little break.

VOICE OF AURORA. What you gonna do for money?

JACK LOVINGTON. I don't know. I'll find something.

VOICE OF AURORA. I'm still working at the flower shop.

JACK LOVINGTON. That's good. We could use it. Diapers cost money. *(After a moment, the door swings open. We see Aurora wearing the wide-brimmed hat. Her face obscured.)*

VOICE OF AURORA. Do you love me? *(The sound of raindrops begin to rise again.)*

JACK LOVINGTON. *(Pause.)* To the moon and back, times infinity. *(Aurora takes off her hat and we see her as Jack does … she's stunning. Jack rushes in. They kiss. The best recorded kiss of 1958. They close the door behind them. Lights out.)*

End of Play

PROPERTY LIST

Bag of groceries, umbrella
Shoes and socks
Cardboard, with "SKATE" carved into it
Microphone
Whistle
Sunglasses
Rosary
Cash
Letters
Powder blue stationery, pen, suitcase, wristwatch
Coat, pocket watch
Keys
Crossword puzzle
Envelopes
Rotgut, suitcases
Stationery, pen
Mouthguard
Mail, filled with blue shredded stationery
Paper
Handkerchief
Paper bag with beer
Champagne and glass
Quarters, pills in bottle
Wallet, picture
Cash in envelope
Blue bag, 2 pill bottles, red bag
Cup of urine
Rubber gloves, needles, syringes, wooden stick
Letter and envelope on red stationery
Pen
Spanish language primer
Flask
Taped together blue love letter

SOUND EFFECTS

Drip hitting bucket
Rock 'n' roll music: guitar and sax
VO 1950s TV announcer
Knock on door
Pigeon wings flapping
Spanish voices, applause
Arena noise, rock 'n' roll
Booing crowd
Rioting crowd
Cheering crowd
1950s orchestral pop, from radio
Beer can pop tops
Car horn
Toilet flush
Bus engine starting
Bus horn
1950s TV show orchestral music
Church music
Roller coaster
Sound of light rain falling
Raindrops hitting bucket
Kissing sound, c. 1958

NEW PLAYS

★ **GUARDIANS by Peter Morris.** In this unflinching look at war, a disgraced American soldier discloses the truth about Abu Ghraib prison, and a clever English journalist reveals how he faked a similar story for the London tabloids. "Compelling, sympathetic and powerful." *–NY Times.* "Sends you into a state of moral turbulence." *–Sunday Times (UK).* "Nothing short of remarkable." *–Village Voice.* [1M, 1W] ISBN: 978-0-8222-2177-7

★ **BLUE DOOR by Tanya Barfield.** Three generations of men (all played by one actor), from slavery through Black Power, challenge Lewis, a tenured professor of mathematics, to embark on a journey combining past and present. "A teasing flare for words." *–Village Voice.* "Unfailingly thought-provoking." *–LA Times.* "The play moves with the speed and logic of a dream." *–Seattle Weekly.* [2M] ISBN: 978-0-8222-2209-5

★ **THE INTELLIGENT DESIGN OF JENNY CHOW by Rolin Jones.** This irreverent "techno-comedy" chronicles one brilliant woman's quest to determine her heritage and face her fears with the help of her astounding creation called Jenny Chow. "Boldly imagined." *–NY Times.* "Fantastical and funny." *–Variety.* "Harvests many laughs and finally a few tears." *–LA Times.* [3M, 3W] ISBN: 978-0-8222-2071-8

★ **SOUVENIR by Stephen Temperley.** Florence Foster Jenkins, a wealthy society eccentric, suffers under the delusion that she is a great coloratura soprano—when in fact the opposite is true. "Hilarious and deeply touching. Incredibly moving and breathtaking." *–NY Daily News.* "A sweet love letter of a play." *–NY Times.* "Wildly funny. Completely charming." *–Star-Ledger.* [1M, 1W] ISBN: 978-0-8222-2157-9

★ **ICE GLEN by Joan Ackermann.** In this touching period comedy, a beautiful poetess dwells in idyllic obscurity on a Berkshire estate with a band of unlikely cohorts. "A beautifully written story of nature and change." *–Talkin' Broadway.* "A lovely play which will leave you with a lot to think about." *–CurtainUp.* "Funny, moving and witty." *–Metroland (Boston).* [4M, 3W] ISBN: 978-0-8222-2175-3

★ **THE LAST DAYS OF JUDAS ISCARIOT by Stephen Adly Guirgis.** Set in a time-bending, darkly comic world between heaven and hell, this play reexamines the plight and fate of the New Testament's most infamous sinner. "An unforced eloquence that finds the poetry in lowdown street talk." *–NY Times.* "A real jaw-dropper." *–Variety.* "An extraordinary play." *–Guardian (UK).* [10M, 5W] ISBN: 978-0-8222-2082-4

DRAMATISTS PLAY SERVICE, INC.
440 Park Avenue South, New York, NY 10016 212-683-8960 Fax 212-213-1539
postmaster@dramatists.com www.dramatists.com

NEW PLAYS

★ **THE GREAT AMERICAN TRAILER PARK MUSICAL music and lyrics by David Nehls, book by Betsy Kelso.** Pippi, a stripper on the run, has just moved into Armadillo Acres, wreaking havoc among the tenants of Florida's most exclusive trailer park. "Adultery, strippers, murderous ex-boyfriends, Costco and the Ice Capades. Undeniable fun." *–NY Post.* "Joyful and unashamedly vulgar." *–The New Yorker.* "Sparkles with treasure." *–New York Sun.* [2M, 5W] ISBN: 978-0-8222-2137-1

★ **MATCH by Stephen Belber.** When a young Seattle couple meet a prominent New York choreographer, they are led on a fraught journey that will change their lives forever. "Uproariously funny, deeply moving, enthralling theatre." *–NY Daily News.* "Prolific laughs and ear-to-ear smiles." *–NY Magazine.* [2M, 1W] ISBN: 978-0-8222-2020-6

★ **MR. MARMALADE by Noah Haidle.** Four-year-old Lucy's imaginary friend, Mr. Marmalade, doesn't have much time for her—not to mention he has a cocaine addiction and a penchant for pornography. "Alternately hilarious and heartbreaking." *–The New Yorker.* "A mature and accomplished play." *–LA Times.* "Scathingly observant comedy." *–Miami Herald.* [4M, 2W] ISBN: 978-0-8222-2142-5

★ **MOONLIGHT AND MAGNOLIAS by Ron Hutchinson.** Three men cloister themselves as they work tirelessly to reshape a screenplay that's just not working—*Gone with the Wind.* "Consumers of vintage Hollywood insider stories will eat up Hutchinson's diverting conjecture." *–Variety.* "A lot of fun." *–NY Post.* "A Hollywood dream-factory farce." *–Chicago Sun-Times.* [3M, 1W] ISBN: 978-0-8222-2084-8

★ **THE LEARNED LADIES OF PARK AVENUE by David Grimm, translated and freely adapted from Molière's Les Femmes Savantes.** Dicky wants to marry Betty, but her mother's plan is for Betty to wed a most pompous man. "A brave, brainy and barmy revision." *–Hartford Courant.* "A rare but welcome bird in contemporary theatre." *–New Haven Register.* "Roll over Cole Porter." *–Boston Globe.* [5M, 5W] ISBN: 978-0-8222-2135-7

★ **REGRETS ONLY by Paul Rudnick.** A sparkling comedy of Manhattan manners that explores the latest topics in marriage, friendships and squandered riches. "One of the funniest quip-meisters on the planet." *–NY Times.* "Precious moments of hilarity. Devastatingly accurate political and social satire." *–BackStage.* "Great fun." *–CurtainUp.* [3M, 3W] ISBN: 978-0-8222-2223-1

DRAMATISTS PLAY SERVICE, INC.
440 Park Avenue South, New York, NY 10016   212-683-8960   Fax 212-213-1539
postmaster@dramatists.com   www.dramatists.com

NEW PLAYS

★ **AFTER ASHLEY by Gina Gionfriddo.** A teenager is unwillingly thrust into the national spotlight when a family tragedy becomes talk-show fodder. "A work that virtually any audience would find accessible." *–NY Times.* "Deft characterization and caustic humor." *–NY Sun.* "A smart satirical drama." *–Variety.* [4M, 2W] ISBN: 978-0-8222-2099-2

★ **THE RUBY SUNRISE by Rinne Groff.** Twenty-five years after Ruby struggles to realize her dream of inventing the first television, her daughter faces similar battles of faith as she works to get Ruby's story told on network TV. "Measured and intelligent, optimistic yet clear-eyed." *–NY Magazine.* "Maintains an exciting sense of ingenuity." *–Village Voice.* "Sinuous theatrical flair." *–Broadway.com.* [3M, 4W] ISBN: 978-0-8222-2140-1

★ **MY NAME IS RACHEL CORRIE taken from the writings of Rachel Corrie, edited by Alan Rickman and Katharine Viner.** This solo piece tells the story of Rachel Corrie who was killed in Gaza by an Israeli bulldozer set to demolish a Palestinian home. "Heartbreaking urgency. An invigoratingly detailed portrait of a passionate idealist." *–NY Times.* "Deeply authentically human." *–USA Today.* "A stunning dramatization." *–CurtainUp.* [1W] ISBN: 978-0-8222-2222-4

★ **ALMOST, MAINE by John Cariani.** This charming midwinter night's dream of a play turns romantic clichés on their ear as it chronicles the painfully hilarious amorous adventures (and misadventures) of residents of a remote northern town that doesn't quite exist. "A whimsical approach to the joys and perils of romance." *–NY Times.* "Sweet, poignant and witty." *–NY Daily News.* "Aims for the heart by way of the funny bone." *–Star-Ledger.* [2M, 2W] ISBN: 978-0-8222-2156-2

★ **Mitch Albom's TUESDAYS WITH MORRIE by Jeffrey Hatcher and Mitch Albom, based on the book by Mitch Albom.** The true story of Brandeis University professor Morrie Schwartz and his relationship with his student Mitch Albom. "A touching, life-affirming, deeply emotional drama." *–NY Daily News.* "You'll laugh. You'll cry." *–Variety.* "Moving and powerful." *–NY Post.* [2M] ISBN: 978-0-8222-2188-3

★ **DOG SEES GOD: CONFESSIONS OF A TEENAGE BLOCKHEAD by Bert V. Royal.** An abused pianist and a pyromaniac ex-girlfriend contribute to the teen-angst of America's most hapless kid. "A welcome antidote to the notion that the *Peanuts* gang provides merely American cuteness." *–NY Times.* "Hysterically funny." *–NY Post.* "The *Peanuts* kids have finally come out of their shells." *–Time Out.* [4M, 4W] ISBN: 978-0-8222-2152-4

DRAMATISTS PLAY SERVICE, INC.
440 Park Avenue South, New York, NY 10016 212-683-8960 Fax 212-213-1539
postmaster@dramatists.com www.dramatists.com

NEW PLAYS

★ **RABBIT HOLE by David Lindsay-Abaire.** Winner of the 2007 Pulitzer Prize. Becca and Howie Corbett have everything a couple could want until a life-shattering accident turns their world upside down. "An intensely emotional examination of grief, laced with wit." *–Variety.* "A transcendent and deeply affecting new play." *–Entertainment Weekly.* "Painstakingly beautiful." *–BackStage.* [2M, 3W] ISBN: 978-0-8222-2154-8

★ **DOUBT, A Parable by John Patrick Shanley.** Winner of the 2005 Pulitzer Prize and Tony Award. Sister Aloysius, a Bronx school principal, takes matters into her own hands when she suspects the young Father Flynn of improper relations with one of the male students. "All the elements come invigoratingly together like clockwork." *–Variety.* "Passionate, exquisite, important, engrossing." *–NY Newsday.* [1M, 3W] ISBN: 978-0-8222-2219-4

★ **THE PILLOWMAN by Martin McDonagh.** In an unnamed totalitarian state, an author of horrific children's stories discovers that someone has been making his stories come true. "A blindingly bright black comedy." *–NY Times.* "McDonagh's least forgiving, bravest play." *–Variety.* "Thoroughly startling and genuinely intimidating." *–Chicago Tribune.* [4M, 5 bit parts (2M, 1W, 1 boy, 1 girl)] ISBN: 978-0-8222-2100-5

★ **GREY GARDENS book by Doug Wright, music by Scott Frankel, lyrics by Michael Korie.** The hilarious and heartbreaking story of Big Edie and Little Edie Bouvier Beale, the eccentric aunt and cousin of Jacqueline Kennedy Onassis, once bright names on the social register who became East Hampton's most notorious recluses. "An experience no passionate theatergoer should miss." *–NY Times.* "A unique and unmissable musical." *–Rolling Stone.* [4M, 3W, 2 girls] ISBN: 978-0-8222-2181-4

★ **THE LITTLE DOG LAUGHED by Douglas Carter Beane.** Mitchell Green could make it big as the hot new leading man in Hollywood if Diane, his agent, could just keep him in the closet. "Devastatingly funny." *–NY Times.* "An out-and-out delight." *–NY Daily News.* "Full of wit and wisdom." *–NY Post.* [2M, 2W] ISBN: 978-0-8222-2226-2

★ **SHINING CITY by Conor McPherson.** A guilt-ridden man reaches out to a therapist after seeing the ghost of his recently deceased wife. "Haunting, inspired and glorious." *–NY Times.* "Simply breathtaking and astonishing." *–Time Out.* "A thoughtful, artful, absorbing new drama." *–Star-Ledger.* [3M, 1W] ISBN: 978-0-8222-2187-6

DRAMATISTS PLAY SERVICE, INC.
440 Park Avenue South, New York, NY 10016 212-683-8960 Fax 212-213-1539
postmaster@dramatists.com   www.dramatists.com